The Recreation Guide
to **WASHINGTON**
NATIONAL FORESTS

by
Wendy Walker

FALCON PRESS®

Helena, Montana

Falcon Press is continually expanding its list of recreational guidebooks using the same general format as this book. All books include detailed descriptions, accurate maps, and all information necessary for enjoyable trips. You can order extra copies of this book and get information and prices for other Falcon books by writing Falcon Press, P.O. Box 1718, Helena, MT 59624. Also, please ask for a free copy of our current catalog listing all Falcon Press books.

ISBN: 1-56044-163-1

Printed in the United States of America.

Falcon Press Publishing Co., Inc.
P.O. Box 1718, Helena, MT 59624

Cover Photo: by Cliff Leight

Library of Congress Cataloging-in-Publication Data:

Walker, Wendy.
    Recreation guide to Washington national forests / by Wendy Walker.
        p.   cm.
      ISBN 1-56044-163-1 (pbk.)
      1. Forest reserves—Washington (State)–Recreational use
    —Guidebooks. 2. National parks and reserves–Washington (State)
    —Recreational use—Guidebooks. 3. Campsites, facilities, etc.
    —Washington (State)—Guidebooks. 4. Washington (State)
    —Guidebooks.
    I. Title.
    GV191.42.W2W35 1992
    333.78'4—dc20
                                                                    92-54597
                                                                    CIP

ACKNOWLEDGMENTS

Thanks to the people from each of the national forests who provided information, answered my questions, and reviewed the text. And thank you to Anita Wahler who proofread and Mac Bates' eighth grade language arts class at Valley View Middle School who helped find errors in the rough draft.

CONTENTS

WASHINGTON NATIONAL FORESTS

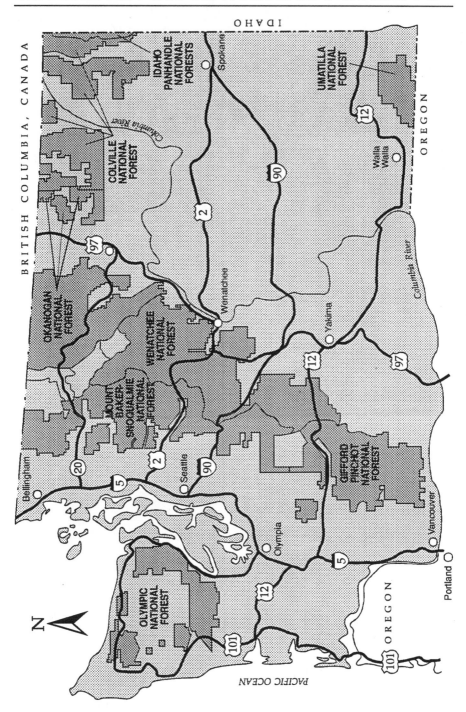

MAP LEGEND

Interstate	(00)	River, Drainage	
U.S. Highway	(00)	Lakes	
State or Other Principle Road	(00)	Wilderness Area	
Forest Road	[000]	National Park	
Paved Road			
Unpaved Road	= = = = = =	National Recreation Area (NRA)	
Trail			
Ranger Station		State Forest	

National Forest Boundary

State Boundary

International Boundary

Indian Reservation Boundary

0   5   10   15
Miles

N

Hiking in Washington's national forests is one of many recreation activities available. Cliff Leight photo.

Table Mountain, Located near the Canadian border in the Mount Baker–Snoqualmie National Forest. Jim Hughes, Forest Service photo.

INTRODUCTION

Overview of Washington National Forests

From the rain forests at the western edge of the state to the dry canyon-cut plateau of the southeast, Washington national forests showcase nature's stunning variety. One national forest may average twelve feet of rain a year and provide habitat for Sitka spruce and Roosevelt elk; another may only have six inches of rain a year and grow lodgepole pine and rattlesnakes.

A series of mountain ranges uplift much of Washington State and the eight national forests correspond to the mountains. The Olympic National Forest covers the lower slopes of the Olympic Mountains at the western edge of Washington. The Mount Baker-Snoqualmie, Gifford Pinchot, Okanogan and Wenatchee national forests blanket the Cascade Range, the north-south spine of the state. The Colville and Idaho Panhandle national forests spread across the slopes of the Selkirk Mountains in the northeast. The Umatilla National Forest includes the canyons and plateaus of the Blue Mountains of southeastern Washington.

More than three-fourths of the glaciers in the continental United States are found in the Cascades and Olympics. Glacial ice covers many of the peaks in these ranges all year. Some of the largest trees and most immense forests in the world grow in Washington national forests. Bald eagles are still common along many rivers, feeding on spawning salmon. Wolves are returning to the northern forests. Grizzly bear, caribou, and moose still roam several of the state's national forests.

The natural wonders of the national forests of Washington provide a setting for a wide array of recreational opportunities. Visitors enjoy scenic drives, camping, picnicking, ranger programs, photography, and berry-picking. Climbers scale rock cliffs and ascend glaciers. Hikers stroll through wildflower meadows, wander among huge old trees, and seek solitude and challenge in wilderness areas.

Hunters stalk deer, elk, bear, and grouse. Anglers catch trout, salmon, and dolly varden from rushing streams and clear mountain lakes. Rafters and kayakers negotiate whitewater rapids and motor boaters explore lowland lakes. Skiers swish down commercial ski runs or glide along cross-country tracks. Snowmobilers enjoy snowy forest roads. Families can play in the snow all year.

Washington national forests offer enough adventure, fascination, serenity, entertainment, and challenge to last a lifetime.

The eight national forests of Washington vary in size and in levels of recreational development. The forests on the western side of the Cascade Mountains are close to the major population centers of Washington and tend to be more crowded and have more developed recreation facilities and access routes.

The western national forests have more rain, thicker forests, and more glaciers than those on the eastern side of the state. This is due to the rainshadow effect of the high Cascade mountains. Storms blowing in off the Pacific Ocean drop most of their moisture on the western slopes of the

Cascades, leaving the eastern side much drier, warmer, and more susceptible to forest fires.

The northernmost national forests were almost totally buried in ice during the last two million years of ice ages. This ice ocean sculpted the craggy peaks, deep cirque lakes, and large U-shaped valleys that characterize the northern mountains. The national forests in the southern part of the state tend to have more rounded mountains and V-shaped river valleys due to less extensive glaciation.

A series of volcanos erupted out of the crest of the Cascade Range during the last million years, creating the tallest, glacier-drenched peaks of the range. Mount Baker, Glacier Peak, Mount Adams, and Mount St. Helens all rise to around 10,000 feet within the national forests of Washington. The tallest volcano, Mount Rainier, at 14,410 feet, lies within Mount Rainier National Park.

Climate can vary remarkably even within a single national forest due to elevation differences of thousands of feet. On a July day a hiker on a mountain ridge at 7,000 feet might be standing on a snow bank, shivering in a forty-degree wind, watching mountain goats graze. Another visitor on the same day, forty miles away and 6,000 feet lower, might be walking in sagebrush, sweating in the eighty-degree sunshine, and watching a rattlesnake slither beneath a rock.

The human history of Washington national forests dates back thousands of years to the times when Native Americans first started living in the mountains. Native Americans harvested salmon, berries, deer, bear, and other foods, and built homes out of cedar trees. A rich ceremonial life accompanied Native American hunting and gathering.

The first non-Indian settlers arrived in the mid-1850s, but the national forest areas never became areas of dense settlement due to their harsh climate and steep terrain. The national forests were set aside in the late 1800s and formally designated in 1905.

National Forest Regulations

The guide for appropriate behavior within Washington national forests might be summed up by advising respect for others, including plants, animals, and other humans. Minimize your impact on the national forests by trying to leave no trace of your visit.

All areas of Washington national forests have some common rules:
- **No littering**
- **Campfires must be extinguished when you leave**
- **Off-road vehicles must be street-legal**
- **Drivers of off-road vehicles must be licensed**
- **Fishing and hunting require licenses**
- **Washington State fishing and hunting regulations apply**
- **Pets must be under control at all times**
- **Firearms may not be used near trails, roads, camps, or lakes**

Accessibility

National forest facilities are being updated to improve accessibility for visitors with mobility, visual, and hearing difficulties. Most buildings and

Barrier-free trails and facilities allow people of many differing abilities to enjoy recreation in the national forests. Jim Hughes, Forest Service photo.

some trails are now accessible for wheelchairs. Newer signs and exhibits have large type, good color contrast, and some raised-relief graphics and text. Audio tapes are available for some interpretive walks and drives. Accessible recreational opportunities will be detailed in each forest chapter.

See the individual national forest chapters for more specific information about barrier-free programs and facilities within each national forest.

Visitor Information Services

Information about each national forest can be obtained by writing or calling ahead of time to the individual forest headquarters or to the district offices. The addresses and phone numbers are listed within each forest's chapter in this book. Free brochures are available and maps of each forest can be purchased for a minimal fee.

Most forests offer visitor information facilities near major forest access points. Often these facilities will be staffed offices along the highway that offer free brochures, sales items such as maps and guidebooks, and employees to answer questions and help plan trips. Some offices also have interactive computers with in-depth information about recreational opportunities.

Visitor information offices are generally open during peak visitor use, usually on weekends and during the summer months. Essential information about the area is also available twenty-four hours a day from outdoor information exhibits at most information offices.

Most information facilities function as administrative centers for campground maintenance, law enforcement, and fire control. Many have climbing

Forest Service information centers are usually located on major access routes into the national forests. Jim Hughes, Forest Service photo.

registers outside to aid in mountain rescue efforts. Some facilities also double as interpretive centers and contain exhibits about the natural and human history of the area.

The sales areas of national forest visitor information offices in Washington are operated by the Northwest Interpretive Association. This nonprofit group offers educational sales items such as field guides, climbing guides, topographic maps, hiking guides, and books on local history, geology, biology, and other topics. Profits from the sales are used to finance publication of books and trail guides, acquisition of materials for exhibits and libraries, field seminar programs, and other projects to enhance visitors' understanding of national forests.

Scenic Drives

The National Forest Scenic Byways in Washington State offer spectacular views, interesting historical and natural features, and interpretive exhibits and programs. Each of the byways was designated for its outstanding visual qualities and the unique experiences it offers.

Many national forests offer a brochure or audio tape guide to scenic byways available from forest service offices. These guides provide route information and interpretive insights into the byways. Interpretive exhibits located along the byways also provide additional information.

Other forest roads may not be designated as formal scenic byways but still offer a multitude of scenic driving opportunities. Some allow travel to out-of-the-way recreational destinations such as lakes and waterfalls. Others allow an overview of the national forest.

Forest roads are often narrow gravel tracks with frequent blind curves. Drivers may encounter logging trucks or other commercial traffic. Drive slowly and carefully.

Interpretive Exhibits and Programs

Many national forests offer roadside and visitor center exhibits as well as self-guided interpretive trails. Some forests also have ranger-guided interpretive walks and demonstrations at high-use areas. Children's programs may also be available. Contact the nearest forest service office for locations and schedules.

Camping

There are more than 500 developed campgrounds in Washington national forests. All campgrounds offer picnic tables, tent pads, fire grates, outhouses, and garbage cans. Some have running water and firewood sales. Some of the larger campgrounds have a live-in volunteer host and may have flush toilets. A few have hook-ups for trailers and motor homes.

Most campgrounds are located near hiking, fishing, interpretive exhibits, swimming, and boating. Some of the largest campgrounds offer interpretive programs during the peak visitor seasons. Some campgrounds are set aside for group use and can be reserved ahead of time by calling the district office nearest the camp area.

Campgrounds with minimal facilities are often free. Others have fees that

Ranger-guided interpretive programs help visitors appreciate the stories behind the scenery. Jim Hughes, Forest Service photo.

vary, depending on the facilities offered, from three dollars to around ten dollars per night. Most campgrounds open around Memorial Day and close around Labor Day. Some low-elevation campgrounds may be open during the winter, with limited services. Some campsites can be reserved ahead of time by calling the Mistix Campground Reservations System, 1-800-283-CAMP. Reservation fees are in addition to the regular campground fee.

Campers can also choose their own camp spot away from developed sites anywhere along the extensive national forest road system. Dispersed camping is legal unless an area is specifically signed "no camping." Dispersed camping rules are designed to prevent damage to the forest.

Each dispersed camping group must carry a gallon water container, a shovel, and an ax for fire control. Existing fire rings should be used when possible for campfires. If a new ring is necessary, it should be built in an opening at least ten feet in diameter. The ground should be cleared to mineral soil. When leaving the campsite, campers should remove all evidence of use, including litter and the campfire ring.

Wildlife

Washington national forests are home to more than 150,000 deer, 30,000 elk, 9,000 black bear, 4,500 mountain goat, and 300 bighorn sheep. Other large mammals such as cougar, coyote, bobcat, lynx, and moose exist in smaller numbers. Grizzly bear, wolf, and caribou are rarely found and are listed as endangered species.

Common birds that can be seen in the national forests include grouse, ptarmigan, varied thrush, water ouzel, and several species of hawk. Endangered species such as bald eagle, spotted owl, and peregrine falcon also live in the national forests.

Watchable wildlife sites have been designated throughout the national forests in areas where wildlife can easily be seen. A guide to the sites is available for sale in most U.S. Forest Service visitor centers. Most animals in the national forest are harmless when viewed from a distance. Stay safe and show respect for wildlife by watching animals quietly, without intruding on their habitat.

Hunting is legal within national forests and is regulated by the Washington State Wildlife Department. Common game species include mule deer, whitetail deer, elk, bear, and grouse. A few permits are sold each year for the less common mountain goat, moose, and bighorn sheep. Most hunting seasons occur in late summer and fall. Terrain is rugged, weather unpredictable and cross-country travel challenging. Hunters should wear warm, sturdy, bright-colored clothing and always carry the ten essentials for backcountry travel.

The most famous fish of the northwest, the salmon, lives most of its life in the ocean but uses the rivers of Washington national forests for spawning and rearing habitat. There are six species: coho, chinook, chum, pink, and sockeye, and each has somewhat different life cycles and habitat needs. Sea-run steelhead and dolly varden also use the rivers for spawning. Resident fish include rainbow and cutthroat trout. There are more than 10,000 miles of fishing streams in Washington national forests.

Fishing seasons vary with the body of water, but most areas are open during the summer months. Fishing is regulated by the Washington State Department of Fisheries. Catch limits and release rules also vary. In-state and out-of-state licenses can be bought along with bait and tackle at many retail outlets near forest boundaries. Fishing regulations are available where licenses are sold.

Foraging

Berries, mushrooms, wildflowers, and floral greens are free for the picking within the national forests as long as they are for home use. Commercial pickers usually must obtain a permit from the Forest Service.

Permits can be obtained for a small fee for firewood, fenceposts, Christmas trees, rocks, and gravel. Availability varies with the season and ecosystem concerns.

When in doubt as to whether a forest product is available for harvest, check with the nearest forest service office for current regulations. When harvesting, take care to reduce damage to the surrounding plants and animals as much as possible.

Commercial Uses of National Forests

National forests were set aside by Congress for multiple uses. Timber harvest, mining, grazing, and other commercial uses are legal within the national forest system. Visitors may encounter logging traffic, see grazing livestock, stumble across a mining claim, or watch commercial mushroom pickers at work.

The Forest Service regulates commercial uses of the national forests, working to maintain the long-term viability of ecosystems. Usually, commercial activities are intentionally located away from major recreation highlights.

Water Recreation

The raging rapids of Washington national forest rivers can provide exhilarating whitewater rafting, kayaking, and canoeing. Only experienced boaters should attempt whitewater rivers. The water is very cold and currents, boulders, and waterfalls pose dangers. Guided raft trips can be purchased from private companies that operate under permit within the national forests.

The many lakes offer flatwater boating. Some of the larger lakes are open to motorized craft. Most lakeside campgrounds provide boat launches. A few campgrounds are only accessible by boat. Some anglers carry inflatable rafts to mountain lakes accessible only by trail.

Swimming in the mountain lakes of the national forests is not for the faint-of-heart. Many lakes are fed by melting glaciers. Water temperatures may hover in the forties. Some lakeside campgrounds provide swimming beaches but no lifeguards.

There's still gold in "them thar hills." Not enough to make anyone rich, but enough for recreational gold panners to find a few flakes in the bottom of a gold pan. Check with ranger offices for good locations and ways to minimize damage to fish spawning nests.

Water Safety

Boaters should always wear life preservers. The water is very cold and strong winds can come up at any time in any season, making a return to dock dangerous. Make sure boats have extra food and clothing aboard for emergencies.

Whitewater rafters and kayakers should wear wetsuits, especially in the spring and fall. Rivers have hidden logs and boulders that can easily overturn a boat. Overhead logs can also cause injuries. Be sure to check out rapids ahead of time before running them. Don't necessarily trust the guidebooks. Floods can change the configuration and power of a rapid at any time.

Swimmers should stay close to shore. Water is very cold and can incapacitate even the strongest swimmers. Parents should watch children in the water at all times. Swimmers should avoid rivers with strong currents; getting swept downstream can be fatal. Many rivers have powerful rapids and waterfalls.

Winter Recreation

Thirteen commercial ski areas operate within Washington national forests, providing downhill ski runs, day lodges, groomed trails for cross-country skiing, and snowplay areas.

Cross-country skiers and snowmobilers can also enjoy hundreds of miles of unplowed roads and trails that are in areas less prone to avalanches. Some areas are designated for skiers only.

The Forest Service designates snowplay areas with plowed parking lots in some national forests. Purchase of a parking permit helps pay for the plowing. Here families can enjoy activities like sliding, snowball fights, and igloo building.

Accurate winter road conditions can be heard twenty-four hours a day by calling the Washington State Department of Transportation mountain pass reporting service at 1-900-407-7277.

Winter Safety

Avalanches, hypothermia, wind chill, frostbite, dehydration, getting lost...A list of the dangers of winter travel is enough to make you stay at home in front of the television. But enjoying the winter in the mountains can be safe and exhilarating if a few simple precautions are kept in mind.

Always carry the ten essentials for hiking. For winter travel add: extra warm clothing; and repair kits for skis, snowshoes, or snowmobile. Always travel with a companion and tell someone when you will be back. Stay dry, eat and drink often, and don't get exhausted.

Avalanches are especially dangerous in the North Cascades and Olympic Mountains. Visitors should check with Forest Service offices for areas that are protected from avalanche and for current avalanche conditions.

Those caught in an avalanche should discard all equipment, make swimming motions, and put their hands in front of their faces to create an air pocket. Someone witnessing an avalanche should mark the place the victim was last seen and probe the snow with a pole directly downslope. If there is only one witness, he or she should stay and search. If there are others, one should go for help while others search. After thirty minutes, the victim has

"Winter" can last into August at high elevations. Jim Hughes, Forest Service photo.

only a fifty-percent chance of survival.

Avalanches are most common on moderate slopes of thirty to forty degrees, on north-facing slopes in winter, on south-facing slopes in spring, on smooth slopes with no trees, and during and after storms with heavy snowfall.

Backcountry Travel

The mountainous terrain of Washington national forests offers unparalleled hiking and climbing. But backcountry travel can be dangerous unless visitors are prepared. The weather can change suddenly during any season. Snow is possible at higher elevations even in August. Avalanches can be lethal during the winter and spring months.

The following ten essential items should be carried at all times in the backcountry:

1. **extra clothing, including rain gear**
2. **extra food**
3. **sunglasses**
4. **pocket knife**
5. **matches in waterproof container**
6. **firestarter—candle, wax paper**
7. **first aid kit**
8. **flashlight**
9. **map**
10.**compass**

Backpackers need to carry gear for personal comfort, emergencies, and reducing impact on fragile ecosystems. Jim Hughes, Forest Service photo.

Washington national forests contain extensive high-elevation trails that stay snow-covered well into mid-summer. An ice-axe and sunglasses are essential for snow travel.

Hikers should not drink water from streams and rivers no matter how far they are from civilization. Microorganisms in the water are spread by wildlife as well as by humans and can cause severe illness. Water should be treated by filtering, chemicals, or boiling.

Backcountry users should check with a Forest Service office for current hiking and trail conditions. Each party should inform someone of its route, camp spots, and approximate return time to help facilitate mountain rescue should it be necessary.

Responsible backcountry hikers should: Wear light boots or running shoes if conditions allow; never cut switchbacks; avoid going around obstacles to create new trails. If traveling off-trail, stick to timber or rocky routes rather than fragile meadows. Subalpine plants are not adapted to human trampling. Please stay on designated trails.

Backcountry campers should: Camp at least 200 feet from any water source and use existing areas when possible. Try to select muted colors that will blend with surroundings. Use established latrines. Otherwise bury human waste at least 200 feet from water, trails, and camps. Wash dishes, clothes, and yourself 200 feet from water. Use biodegradable soap or none at all. Pack out what you packed in and anything you find that others have left.

Mountain Climbing

Climbers scale sheer rock walls, maneuver in and out of glacial crevasses, and scramble cross-country along miles and miles of alpine ridges in Washington national forests. People come from all over the world to meet the climbing challenges posed by the Washington mountain ranges.

All climbing groups should include an experienced leader and be equipped appropriately for the terrain. Ropes, ice-axes, and crampons are necessary for snow and ice-climbs year-round. Glacier climbers should always be roped up. Spring climbers should be wary of melting snow bridges over glacial crevasses and streams. Winter climbers should be prepared for frequent avalanches. Commercial guides can be hired by inexperienced groups.

Climbers can sign in at Forest Service visitor centers and then sign out after they climb. The climbing registers are available twenty-four hours a day. Mountain rescue units search for missing climbers based on register information.

Climbing guidebooks for Washington State mountain ranges are available at Forest Service sales areas. Forest Service employees often have up-to-date climbing conditions reported by previous climbing parties.

Special Areas

Some special areas within the national forests are set aside for specific types of recreation. These areas often have different rules regarding recreation use.

Wilderness areas were legislated by Congress for preservation of untamed lands. Hikers should expect to be challenged by rugged terrain and minimal trails, bridges, and signs. The twenty-three wilderness areas within national forests in Washington State encompass a total of five million acres and are accessed by 7,000 miles of trails.

The following use-rules help preserve the primitive and pristine state of wilderness areas:

1. **Only twelve people and eight head of stock in a party**
2. **No motorized vehicles**
3. **Pack out all litter**
4. **Use mountain toilets or bury human waste**

Some highly used or especially fragile locations within wilderness areas may restrict numbers of visitors and require a permit. Campfires are prohibited in many areas above timberline.

National recreation areas offer outstanding and unique recreational opportunities. The only NRA in Washington State is the Mount Baker National Recreation Area on the southeastern slopes of Mount Baker in the Mount Baker-Snoqualmie National Forest.

Research Natural Areas include ecosystems that are undisturbed except by scientific research projects. Generally recreation use of these areas is restricted to reduce impact on the natural systems and to avoid interference with research.

Wild and Scenic Rivers are rivers with clean, free-flowing stretches that have been inducted into the national "hall of fame of rivers" by their Wild and Scenic designation. These rivers support teeming populations of fish and

Climbers from around the world venture into Washington's national forests to test their skills on Washington's mountain ranges. Cliff Leight photo.

wildlife. Recreational uses such as wildlife viewing, birdwatching, rafting, picnicking, and camping are encouraged as long as users respect and help maintain the rivers' pristine qualities.

Historic Districts are areas where outstanding historical resources provide windows into the fascinating past of the national forests. Interpretive signs, programs, archaeology digs, and old buildings help tell the stories of the old days.

How to Get to the National Forests

Driving

Interstate 5 is the major north-south highway into Washington State west of the Cascade Mountains. This four-lane, limited access highway enters Washington from the south at Vancouver and then passes just to the west of the Gifford Pinchot National Forest and just to the east of the Olympic National Forest. From Seattle north to the Canadian border, the interstate skirts the western edge of the Mount Baker-Snoqualmie National Forest.

Highway 97 in eastern Washington runs along the eastern edge of the Cascade mountains from the Washington-Oregon border to the Canadian border. It passes to the east of the Gifford Pinchot, Wenatchee and Okanogan National Forests. Highway 395 and several state routes south from Interstate 90 provide access to the Umatilla National Forest.

East-west routes across Washington State pass through several of the national forests. These routes tend to cross mountain ranges and may require snow tires or chains in the winter. Highway 12 connects Interstate 5 with the city of Yakima and passes just to the north of the Gifford Pinchot National Forest. Interstate 90 connects Seattle to Spokane and passes through the Mount Baker-Snoqualmie and Wenatchee national forests. Highway 2 connects Everett with Wenatchee and also travels through the Mount Baker-Snoqualmie and Wenatchee national forests. Highway 20 connects Anacortes with Newport and the Idaho border and passes through the Mount Baker-Snoqualmie, Okanogan and Colville national forests and near the Idaho Panhandle National Forests.

Paved highways enter each of the national forests in several locations. Paved and gravel forest roads then branch off of the highways to allow further travel. Some areas are unroaded such as wilderness areas and roadless areas and some portions of a national forest may be closed to vehicle access to protect wildlife habitat or for other forest management activities.

Air Travel

The main air portal to Washington State is the Sea-Tac International Airport located between the cities of Seattle and Tacoma. The airport offers flights to all major cities in the United States and flights or connections to flights throughout the world. The Sea-Tac Airport is within easy driving distance of the Olympic, Gifford Pinchot, Mount Baker-Snoqualmie,and Wenatchee national forests.

The Spokane Airport also offers flights to some major cities and air shuttle service to Sea-Tac. The Spokane Airport is within an easy driving distance of the Colville and Idaho Panhandle national forests.

Commuter planes also fly into Wenatchee, Bellingham, Port Angeles, Yakima, Pasco, Walla Walla and Pullman. Car rentals are available at each airport.

Bus Travel

Bus service to the national forests is limited due to the isolated location of most forests. Some commercial bus routes pass through national forests on major highways.

Bus tours from major cities include visits to some national forests. Contact the individual national forest headquarters for more specific information.

Train Travel

Amtrak offers passenger train service east-west through Washington State. The train route connects Spokane with Seattle and passes through portions of the Wenatchee and Mount Baker-Snoqualmie national forests. North-south Amtrak service between Portland, Oregon and the Canadian border is proposed for the mid-1990s, and the route would pass close to the Gifford Pinchot, Olympic, and Mount Baker-Snoqualmie national forests.

How to Use This Book

The following pages list the recreation opportunities available in the national forests of Washington. The first section provides an overview of all the national forests with general descriptions of recreational activities and regulations that are common to all forests.

The subsequent sections provide more detailed and specific information, photographs, and maps for each national forest. The national forest chapters each have camping and recreational highlights information divided by ranger district.

The addresses and phone numbers for each national forest are listed in each chapter. Contact each national forest directly for current conditions and up-to-date information on fees, road closures, and other information that can change rapidly.□

View Southwest from Slate Peak. Sheela McLean photo.

The Thirteen Mile Roadless Area offers miles of hiker and horse trails.
Forest Service photo.

COLVILLE NATIONAL FOREST

The northeastern part of Washington State is often called "the forgotten corner" because it is so far from urban areas. Those who have discovered the memorable wildness, beauty, and rich history of the Colville National Forest may want to change the nickname. Perhaps "the unforgettable corner" is more appropriate.

The Colville National Forest includes three north-south waves of mountains separated by troughs of river valleys. The Kettle, Okanogan, and Selkirk mountain ranges are considered foothills of the Rocky Mountains. Rivers in the troughs between the mountains channel water into the Columbia River, which travels across Washington State to the Pacific Ocean.

The 1.1 million acres of the national forest are known for rolling wooded slopes ranging from lodgepole pine forests to extensive groves of western redcedar. Recreation facilities tend to be rustic and pleasantly uncrowded except on weekends during the summer months.

Location

The national forest nestles in the northeastern corner of Washington State, bordered on the east by Idaho and on the north by Canada. The Okanogan National Forest lies just to the west, the Idaho Panhandle National Forests to the east, and the Colville Indian Reservation to the south.

The closest city is Spokane, Washington, located forty miles south on State Highway 395, a two-lane, paved highway that also runs north to Canada. The city of Coeur d'Alene, Idaho, lies twenty miles east of Spokane along Interstate 90.

Visitors from western Washington and Idaho drive to the national forest from the east and west along State Highway 20, an east-west scenic byway through the national forest.

Climate

The western portions of the national forest are very dry, with desert-like conditions in places. Low rainfall brings frequent fires that perpetuate young lodgepole pine forests. These forests once burned naturally every eight to ten years before human fire control efforts.

Sun shines often in the forest. Temperatures in the summer vary from seventy to 100 degrees in the daytime and from forty to sixty degrees at night. Winter temperatures can dip below zero but usually hover around freezing at lower elevations.

Geology

The northeastern corner of Washington was buried by ice-age glaciers several times during the last two million years. These oceans of ice, thousands of feet thick, ground off the sharp edges of the mountains, leaving the rolling terrain we see today. The glaciers filled valleys, gouging them deeper and wider. When the glaciers retreated to the north, they left behind the topographic features you can see throughout the national forest: gentle south-

COLVILLE NATIONAL FOREST

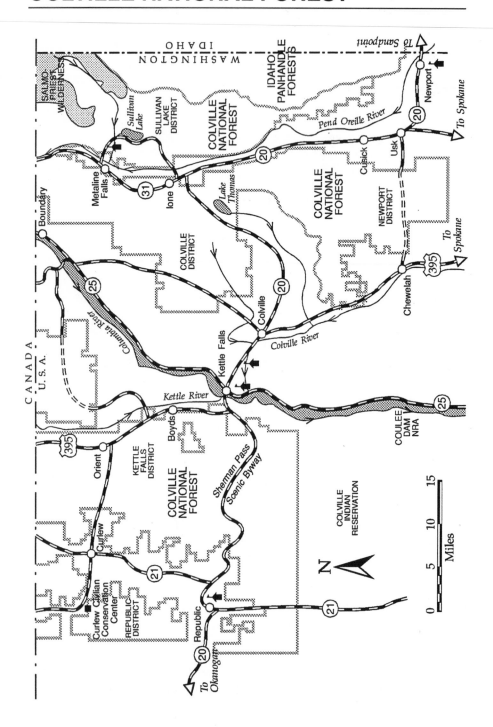

facing slopes, steep north faces and the north-south troughs between the mountain ranges.

Prior to 100 million years ago, the area that is now the Colville National Forest was a flat plain, partially flooded by shallow, inland seas. The sea floors accumulated countless layers of shells and other sediments as organisms died, forming thick deposits of limestone and sandstone. Few if any mountains existed during the 300 million years of inland seas.

During the time of the dinosaurs, around 100 million years ago, a mass of hot, molten rock began to rise beneath western North America. The mass lifted, stretched, and heated the twenty-five mile thick crust, breaking it up into long, narrow blocks that generally ran north-south. During the uplift, great slabs of sandstones and limestones slid down to form jagged peaks such as those found today in Glacier National Park in Montana.

Today, you can see the results of this time of upheaval in the rocks of the Colville National Forest. Coarse-grained, pinkish granite underlies much of the eastern half of the national forest. This rock is the cooled remains of the 100-million-year-old molten mass of rock. Geologists call it the Kaniksu Batholith. The once-flat layers of marine sediment that were intruded by the batholith now tilt at all angles in a complicated jumble that can be seen east of the Columbia River.

In the western half of the national forest, veins of gold and silver penetrate some of the cracks and fissures of sediments and volcanic rock. Historic prospectors searched the area for riches, and mineral exploration continues today near the town of Republic, in the eastern part of the national forest.

The mountains are still rising as earthquakes move these fault-block peaks upward. Volcanos still erupt further west in the Cascade Mountains. The ash-fall from Cascade eruptions forms volcanic soils throughout the Colville National Forest.

Ecology

A variety of ecosystems can be found within the national forest from the dry lodgepole pine forests west of Colville to old-growth cedar east of Sullivan Lake. Many plants and animals are similar to those in the Rocky Mountains to the east. The national forest hosts thirty-four species of sensitive plants that grow mostly in wetlands, bogs, or stream banks.

Much of northeastern Washington burned in forest fires between 1910 and 1930, so many of the trees within the national forest are between seventy and 100 years old. Fire suppression has lengthened natural fire cycles that once ranged from eight to ten years.

A hundred years ago huge natural meadows of camas blossoms could be found in northeastern Washington. The bulb of the camas plant was the main source of carbohydrate for Indians in the region. Kalispel legend tells of scouts who once mistook a valley for a huge lake because it was so thick with blue camas blossoms. Trees have encroached on the camas meadows because of human suppression of wildfire and non-Indian farming.

Human activities have markedly changed ecosystems in northeastern Washington over the last 100 years. Extensive tracts of old-growth conifers used to grow throughout the national forest. Subalpine fir and other evergreens grew at higher elevations and western white pine, larch, grand fir, ponderosa pine, and some Douglas fir grew at mid-elevations.

A small parasite called white pine blister rust has destroyed almost all the western white pine in Washington State in the last 100 years. The blister rust was accidentally imported from Europe. Unlike their European cousins, western white pine have little resistance, and trees almost always die when infected.

Fire and timber harvest also played important roles in changing forest ecosystems. Before fire suppression, low-intensity ground fires burned frequently through pine forests killing young Douglas fir and understory species. Today, Douglas fir is the predominant species in northeastern Washington due to fire control.

Douglas fir is more susceptible to root diseases and insects than are many other tree species. Nearly two million acres of Douglas fir and true firs are under siege by spruce budworm, a native moth that kills host trees by defoliation. You may see large tracts of brown trees dying because of spruce budworm.

Foresters and biologists are trying to restore diverse forest ecosystems within the national forest by planting ponderosa pine, strains of western white pine that are resistant to blister rust, and other insect- and disease-resistant trees.

Another side effect of fire suppression can be seen in the crowded stands of lodgepole pine within the national forest. Older lodgepole stands are often infected with insects or disease. Lodgepole grow on drier slopes of the mountains, usually in single-species forests. Fire naturally clears away the diseased and stunted older trees, allowing younger, more vigorous trees to grow. Also, some lodgepole cones are so tightly sealed with resin that only the heat of fire can free the seeds.

History

The great salmon runs of the Columbia River attracted people to the area we now call the Colville National Forest many thousands of years ago. Archaeologists estimate that Indians caught more than 1,000 salmon a day at Kettle Falls on the Columbia River during peak runs. Salmon congregated below this wide, low falls on their way upstream to spawn.

Some tribes fished and then traveled home with dried fish to villages in other parts of eastern Washington and Idaho. Other tribes lived in the area all year, wintering on the banks of the rivers. The Kalispel people, east of the falls, included in their territory some of the richest camas fields in the region. Baked and dried camas were important food sources in the traditional diet of people worldwide. Remains of camas ovens found at Pioneer Park along the Pend Oreille River date back more than 3,000 years. A trail interpreting Indian lifestyles near the campground interprets the ancient Indian village and the camas baking site.

Fur trappers, miners and homesteaders came later to tap other resources such as fur-bearing animals, timber, and gold. The Hudson's Bay Company established a fur trading post at Fort Colville in 1825. Gold was discovered in 1855, leading the way for prospectors. Homesteaders and timber harvesters came later, seeking homes and livelihoods.

Today, old cabins, empty mining shafts, and abandoned trails provide reminders of the past and await your discovery along windy ridges and within wooded canyons. History is interpreted along the Sherman Pass Scenic Byway west of Kettle Falls along Highway 20. Prehistoric Indian lifestyles are interpreted at Sherman Pass. Other sites such as the Log Flume Interpretive Trail and the Camp Growden Interpretive Site near Kettle Falls provide interpretive windows into the early twentieth century history.

Sullivan Lake near Metaline Falls showcases the history of the northeastern corner of the national forest with an interpretive trail along the remains of a gigantic 2.5-mile-long log flume built in 1910. The flume provided water power for the townsite of Metaline Falls and allowed economic development, including a cement plant. Some of the buildings at the ranger station are good examples of the work of the Civilian Conservation Corps, a 1930s federal work program.

Forest-wide Recreation Opportunities

Scenic Drives

Sherman Pass Scenic Byway—A two-lane paved road, part of State Highway 20 between Republic and Kettle Falls, winds through the Kettle Range to Sherman Pass, the highest pass kept open in the winter in the state of Washington. Panoramic views of undisturbed forests and mountains. The byway offers interpretive exhibits on the history and culture of Native Americans, recent wildfires, early settlers, mining, and forest management.

Wilderness areas

Salmo-Priest Wilderness—30,616 acres within the Colville National Forest include old-growth cedar and hemlock forests and treeless alpine cliffs. It is home to the endangered grizzly bear and caribou.

Special Areas

Thirteen-Mile Roadless Area—This remote backcountry area offers steep, rocky, and pine-covered terrain for exploration.

Wildlife

Mountain caribou, moose, wolf, lemming, and grizzly bear live in the northeastern corner of the Colville National Forest. The U.S. Fish and Wildlife Service lists two threatened species, the bald eagle and the grizzly bear, and three endangered species, the caribou, wolf, and peregrine falcon, within the national forest. Recovery plans are in effect for the grizzly, caribou, bald eagles, and peregrine falcons.

The mountain caribou in the Selkirk Mountains are the last remaining herd in the continental United States. In the late 1980s, less than thirty animals remained. Since then, some caribou from similar ecosystems in British Columbia have been transplanted to increase the numbers and genetic diversity of the herd.

Scientists estimate that ten to twenty grizzly bear still roam the Selkirks. Wildlife managers believe that the population should increase to a viable level if the bears are protected from human-caused mortality and appropriate habitat is maintained.

Rocky Mountain Bighorn Sheep enjoying a midwinter rest at the Noisy Creek Sheep Feeding Station near Sullivan Lake. Forest Service photo.

Mountain goats from the Cascade Mountains were introduced to the Linton Mountain area in the early 1960s. These bearded, white members of the antelope family are protected from hunting in their rocky cliff habitat, and wildlife managers are monitoring their populations and habitat because numbers are low.

Other mammals within the national forest include: pine marten, wolverine, mountain lion, bobcat, shrew, bat, pika, hare, marmot, squirrel, chipmunk, northern pocket gopher, beaver, northern bog lemming, vole, rat, mice, porcupine, coyote, fox, badger, and lynx.

Reptiles and amphibians within the national forest include: Northern long-toed salamander, northwestern tiger salamander, great basin spadefoot toad, Pacific tree frog, western leopard frog, western spotted frog, western painted turtle, northern alligator lizard, western skink, wandering garter snake, western yellow-bellied racer, great basin gopher snake, northern Pacific rattlesnake, and bullfrog.

Birds found in the national forest include: common loon, red-necked grebe, great blue heron, white pelican, whistling swan, Canada goose, blue-winged teal, wood duck, common goldeneye duck, bufflehead, common merganser, turkey vulture, goshawk, red-tailed hawk, Swainson's hawk, golden eagle, marsh hawk, osprey, gyrfalcon, peregrine falcon, grouse, ptarmigan, sandhill crane, killdeer, sandpiper, seagull, dove, snowy owl, barred owl, great horned owl, great gray owl, swift, hummingbird, woodpecker, swallow, brown creeper, wren, thrush, blackbird, finch, yellow-shafted flicker, sparrow, and many species of warbler.

Hunting
Some of the best hunting in the state is within the Colville National Forest. About 60,000 of the state's 90,000 white-tailed deer live in northeast Washington—a fact that has led to one of the longest deer hunting seasons and one of the highest success ratios in the nation. Hunters also stalk black bear, mountain lion, grouse, and elk, and a few lottery winners hunt moose and bighorn sheep each year.

Fishing
Cutthroat, rainbow, German brown, and eastern brook trout populate many high-country lakes, low-elevation lakes, and streams. Lake Roosevelt also contains walleye, sturgeon, and kokanee salmon.

Foraging
The western hemlock and cedar forests of the eastern part of the national forest offer good berry picking opportunities for huckleberries, salmon berries, and thimble berries during the midsummer.

Mushrooms can be gathered for home use in the spring and fall. Permits are required for commercial gathering.

Firewood cutting is permitted within the national forest. Be sure to cut only dead trees lying on the ground. Standing snags are important for wildlife habitat and should not be cut. Small amounts of wood can be gathered free for campground use. Several cords may be gathered for household use with a permit. Permits can be obtained for a small fee from any forest service office.

Water Recreation
Sullivan Lake, Roosevelt Lake, Pend Oreille River, the Pend Oreille Lakes, and other smaller lakes in the national forest offer boating, waterskiing, and swimming along with lakeside camping and picnicking.

Roosevelt Lake, a large reservoir near the national forest, also offers boating, waterskiing, swimming, and rental houseboats.

The Kettle River provides exciting rafting and innertubing opportunities between the Orient Bridge and the Boulder Deer Creek Road Cutoff. Contact U.S. Forest Service offices for more specific directions.

Winter Recreation

Downhill Skiing
The 49 Degrees North Ski Area at Chewelah Mountain has four chairlifts, 1,845-vertical feet drop, and a variety of slopes.

Cross-country Skiing
The national forest has sixty miles of marked and groomed ski trails including Nelson-Calispell, Boulder-Deer Creek Summit, Crater Lake, and Geophysical. Another 300 miles of ungroomed trails await the more adventurous.

Snowmobiling

There are more than 370 miles of signed trails including Lake Butte-Kelly Mountain, King's Lake-South Baldy, Paupac-LeClerc Creek, and Quartz Mountain-Eagle Rock.

Off-road Vehicles and Mountain Bikes

Mountain bikes and motorcycles can use more than 200 miles of trails in the Batey-Bould Area, the Little Pend Oreille Area, and the Taylor Ridge-Twin Sisters Area. All roads and trails in the national forest are open to off-road vehicles unless posted otherwise.

One good trip is the **Indian Creek Trail.** Take Highway 395 a half mile north of Addy and take the two-track road to the right up to the forest boundary and trailhead. This old jeep road is just over three miles long and steep and rocky in places. The trail climbs to Iron Mountain Road on the ridge. The trip features nice vistas and stands of ponderosa pine and Douglas fir.

Backcountry Travel

Hikers and horseback riders can enjoy around 470 miles of horse trails and 510 miles of hiker trails in the Kettle Crest, Abercrombie-Hooknose Area, Thirteen-Mile Roadless Area, and the Selkirk Mountains. The Old State Trail, an old wagon road, is also available between Albian Hill and Lambert Creek. It connects to the Kettle Crest National Recreation Trail.

49 Degrees North Ski Area near Chewelah provides lifts and downhill runs.
Forest Service photo.

U.S. Forest Service information stations offer complete listings of trail opportunities. The examples below just give a taste of what is available.

Non-wilderness Trails

Noisy Creek Trail—From Sullivan Lake Ranger Station proceed four miles south on County Road 9345 to Noisy Creek Campground entrance. Turn left, then turn right at first junction and follow road for 150 yards to trailhead. It is a steep trail up Hall Mountain with great views down to Sullivan Lake. Fourteen miles roundtrip. Open to hikers, horses, and mountain bikes.

Sherlock Peak Trail—Take Silver Creek Road 4720 east from Leadpoint to Forest Road 070 to Forest Road 075 to trailhead. Just over one mile of wooded trail displays panoramic views of the Columbia River Valley, Deep Creek drainage, and surrounding countryside. Small stream and dispersed campsites at trailhead. Huckleberries and wildflowers. Hikers and horses only.

Wilderness Trails

Crowell Ridge Trail—From Sullivan Lake take County Road 9345 north to 2212. Turn right and drive three miles, then turn left onto Forest Road 245 (not recommended for passenger cars). Trail leaves road at switchback 0.75 mile below Sullivan Mountain Lookout. Trail runs along ridge for more than seven miles within the Salmo-Priest Wilderness. Views of small, steep, rocky basins showing evidence of glacial action. Water is scarce. Motorized vehicles are prohibited on all wilderness trails.

Shedroof Divide Trail—East from Sullivan Lake on Nordman-Metaline Road 22. Trail leaves road 0.5 mile beyond Pass Creek Pass. This National Recreation Trail is twenty-two miles one-way, sixteen miles of which lie within the Salmo-Priest Wilderness, with the remainder in proposed wilderness. Most of the trail follows ridges and features substantial elevation changes. Scenic vistas at Round Top, Thunder, and Shedroof mountains. Open to hikers and horses.

Horse Trails

Most trails within the national forest are open to horses and the rolling terrain makes great riding country.

Jungle Hill Trail—Follow Highway 395 from Kettle Falls to Highway 20. Turn left and go twenty miles to the Albian Hill Road 2030. Go north for 0.5 mile to trail sign. Trail climbs steeply for four miles to panoramic views to the east. Access to the Kettle Crest Trail. Horses, mountain bikes, and hikers only.

Mountain Climbing

The Selkirk Mountains within the Salmo-Priest Wilderness Area offer some rock climbing challenges in the summer and snowy ascents in the winter.

Granite outcroppings near Douglas Falls, north of Colville, are popular with rock climbers.

Barrier-Free Sites

All information stations and many campgrounds and restrooms have barrier-free access.

The Millpond Interpretive Trail near Sullivan Lake allows visitors with a wide variety of abilities to enjoy the easy mile-long loop with interpretive signs at historic structures. A bridge spans the top of a modern concrete dam located in the same spot as a 1910 wooden dam that created the millpond.

The Pioneer Interpretive Trail and Wolf Trail are both barrier-free.

Canyon Creek Campground in the Kettle Falls District offers barrier-free hiking and fishing opportunities.

Children's Activities

Children enjoy water sports in the summer and viewing the mountain sheep in the winter at Sullivan Lake.

Interpretive trails like the Millpond Interpretive Trail near Sullivan Lake and the Log Flume Trail near Kettle Falls offer environmental and historical education.

Forest Headquarters

Colville National Forest Headquarters, 765 S. Main St., Colville, Wash., 99114, (509) 684-3711.

Spokane Information Office, 400 South Jefferson, Suite 106, Spokane, Wash., 99204-3142, (509) 353-2574.

Ranger District Recreation Opportunities

Colville Ranger District

The Columbia River bounds the district on the west. The eastern boundary follows a main ridge line between the Columbia and Pend Oreille rivers. Some of the national forest's most popular lakes and trails can be found within the rolling mountains of the district.

Information Centers

Colville Ranger Station, 755 South Main St., Colville, Wash., 99114, (509) 684-4557. Staffed information desk, map and book sales, and restrooms.

Recreation Highlights

Little Pend Oreille Recreation Area—A system of trails along Tiger Highway between Colville and Ione. Offers cross-country skiing, hiking, camping, and picnicking. Off-road vehicle trails are nearby and a system of eight glacial lakes and a navigable waterway offer boating, sailing, fishing, and swimming.

Big Meadow Lake Self-Guided Environmental Education Tour—Numbered stops along an interpretive trail correspond with environmental education activities explained in a guide book that can be checked out from the Colville Ranger Station. Equipment needed for the activities and teacher manuals can also be checked out. Great for families or school classes.

49 Degrees North Downhill Skiing Resort—Offers lifts and downhill ski runs during the winter months. Near Chewelah, south of Colville.

Children from a Colville daycare center plant a tree with a Forest Service interpreter on Arbor Day. Forest Service photo.

South Mill Auto Tour—Self-guided eight-mile auto tour emphasizing ecosystem management. Contact Colville Ranger Station for more information.

Campgrounds

Lake Leo—Twenty-three miles east of Colville via State Highway 20. Eight tent/trailer units and drinking water. Cross-country skiing, swimming, boating, fishing, and off-road vehicle trails. Elevation 3,200 feet. Fee.

Lake Thomas—Twenty miles east of Colville via State Highway 20 and Forest Road 4987. Fifteen tent units and drinking water. Fishing. Elevation 3,200 feet. Fee.

Big Meadow Lake—Twenty-one miles northeast of Colville via County Road 9435 and Forest Road 2695. Sixteen campsites, drinking water, and restrooms. Wheelchair-accessible fishing dock, barrier-free trails, boat ramp, wildlife viewing platform, and self-guided environmental education tour.

Gillette/Lake Gillette—Two campgrounds near each other twenty miles east of Colville via State Highway 20. Six picnic sites, forty-three tent/trailer units, five multiple-family sites, and drinking water. Fishing, interpretive trail, picnicking, boating, and off-road motorcycle trails. Elevation 3,200 feet. Fee.

Little Twin Lakes—Eighteen miles northeast of Colville via County Road 4939 and Forest Road 94B. Twenty tent-trailer units, RVs to sixteen feet, and drinking water. High clearance vehicles only. Fishing. Elevation 3,900 feet.

Resorts and Businesses

Beaver Creek Lodge—Twenty miles east of Colville on Tiger Highway, part of Highway 20. Groceries, restaurant, gas, cabins, camping sites, fishing licenses and supplies, boat rentals.

Colville Chamber of Commerce—995 S. Main St., Colville, Wash., 99114, (509) 684-3517.

Fishing can be a family affair at one of the many safe and accessible lakes within the Colville National Forest. Forest Service photo.

Kettle Falls Ranger District

The Kettle Falls Ranger District lies between the Kettle Crest and the Columbia River. It is bordered on the north by Canada and on the south by the Colville Indian Reservation. The district encompasses many high-elevation habitats, fire-originated ecosystems, and historic sites and trails.

Information Centers

Kettle Falls Ranger Station, 255 West 11th, Kettle Falls, Wash., 99141, (509) 738-6111. Staffed information desk, map and book sales, and restrooms.

Recreation Highlights

Log Flume Heritage Site—A 0.5-mile, barrier-free, easy gravel trail just east of Kettle Falls off Highway 20. Trail suited to street shoes. Interpretive signs along the trail tell about 1920s logging: horses pulling logs, flumes moving logs to mills, and steam locomotives.

Sherman Pass Scenic Byway—Variety of scenic, historic, and recreational opportunities including Camp Growden, a restored CCC camp which now serves as a rest stop. Accesses Kettle Crest and other trailheads, Sherman Pass Native American Trail Route, and the eight-mile-long Old State Wagon Trail, the only wagon trail in the Forest Service trail system.

Campgrounds

Pierre Lake—Twenty miles north of Kettle Falls via State Highway 395 and County Road 4013. Nine picnic sites, fifteen tent/trailer sites, and drinking water. Fishing, boating, and hiking. Elevation 2,100 feet. Fee.

Davis Lake—Sixteen miles northwest of Kettle Falls via State Highway 395 and Forest Road 480. Four tent/trailer units, RVs to sixteen feet, and boat launch. Fishing. Elevation 4,500 feet.

Trout Lake—Fourteen miles west of Kettle Falls via State Highway 20 and Forest Road 20. Four tent/trailer units and drinking water. Fishing, boating, hiking (Hoodoo Canyon Trail 17 to Deadman Creek), and swimming. Elevation 3,000 feet.

Kettle Range—Twenty miles west of Kettle Falls via State Highway 20. Seven picnic sites, nine tent/trailer units, and drinking water. Hiking, viewing area, picnicking. Elevation 5,300 feet.

Canyon Creek—Eight miles west of Kettle Falls via U.S. Highway 395 and State Highway 20. Twelve tent/trailer units and drinking water. Barrier-free trails and fishing platforms. Hiking. Elevation 2,200 feet.

Lake Ellen—Fifteen miles southwest of Kettle Falls via U.S. Highway 395, State Highway 20 and County Road 412. Eleven tent/trailer units and drinking water. Boating and fishing. Elevation 2,300 feet.

Wapaloosie Trailhead and Forest Camp—Twenty-four miles east of Kettle Falls via State Highway 20 and Forest Road 2030. Five rustic campsites. Hitching rails, stock loading ramps, tie stalls with feeders, and stock water. Parking and vault toilets.

Kettle Crest Trailhead and Forest Camp—Sherman Pass Scenic Byway. Three rustic campsites. Hitching rails, stock ramp, parking, vault toilets, and stock water.

The Log Flume Heritage Site Trail, located near Kettle Falls, interprets the history of early logging. Forest Service photo.

Other Campgrounds
National Park Service—Old Kettle Falls Campground, Kettle Falls, Wash.

Resorts and Businesses
Kettle Falls, population 1,300. Stores, restaurants, gas stations.

Kettle Falls Marina— Boat rentals, houseboats, Kettle Falls, Wash.

Grandview Motel and RV Park, Kettle Falls, Wash.

Kettle Falls Chamber of Commerce, 205 E. 3rd, Kettle Falls, Wash., 99141, (509) 738-6444.

Colville, eleven miles south of Kettle Falls, is a full-service community with groceries, gas, laundromat, and restaurants.

Newport Ranger District

The Newport Ranger District lies in the southeast corner of the national forest, close to Spokane and Coeur d'Alene. Patchwork land ownership makes this district a mosaic of public and private land.

Information Centers
99156, (509) 447-3129. Staffed information desk, map and book sales, and restrooms.

Recreation Highlights
Abandoned Homesteads—Hundreds of decaying cabins and abandoned fields dot the Newport Ranger District, reminders of a late homesteading era from 1910 to 1940. Most of the farms failed and were purchased by the federal government.

Pioneer Park Archaeological Site—Indian house pits, storage pits, and charcoal ovens used more than 3,000 years ago by Indians to cook camas bulbs. Interpretive site.

Geophysical Snowpark—Five miles of ski trail loops of varying degrees of difficulty. Access by the Indian Creek Road.

49 Degrees North Cross Country Ski Trail System—Trailheads originate at the 49 Degrees North Ski Area atop Chewelah Mountain, seven miles east of Chewelah, Washington.

Batey-Bould Motorcycle Trail System—Thirty-eight miles of motorcycle trails that connect to the north with the Little Pend Oreille ORV Trail System. Trails access spectacular views, challenging routes, and old homestead sites with interpretive signs. ORVs must have a permit tab if not licensed for highway use, and each vehicle must have a spark-arresting muffler for fire prevention.

Lookouts—Two fire lookouts remain standing, reminiscent of the past. One is on South Baldy and is still staffed by volunteers. The other at Timber Mountain is closed. Both lookouts can be reached via forest roads.

Campgrounds
Panhandle—Fifteen miles north of Usk via County Road 9325. Eleven tent/trailer units, boat launch, and drinking water. Fishing. Located along the

South Baldy Lookout, in the Newport Ranger District, can be reached by driving forest roads and is staffed seasonally by volunteers. Forest Service photo.

Pend Oreille River. Elevation 2,000 feet. Fee.

Brown's Lake—Thirty-two miles north of Newport via County Road 9325. Eighteen tent/trailer units, boat launch, and drinking water. Hiking and fly fishing only. Elevation 3,400 feet. Fee.

South Skookum Lake—Twenty miles north of Newport via County Roads 9325 and 3389. Twenty-four tent/trailer units, boat launch, and drinking water. Fishing and hiking. Elevation 3,500 feet. Fee.

Pioneer Park—2.5 miles north of Newport via County Road 9305. Nine picnic units, twelve tent/trailer units, boat launch, and drinking water. Fishing in Box Canyon Reservoir and hiking. Elevation 2,000 feet. Fee.

Batey-Bould Trailhead—Twenty-four miles north of Newport on Highway 20, then follow signs. Nine fire rings. Toilet facilities and water.

Other campgrounds

North Skookum Lake Campground—Twenty miles north of Newport via County Roads 9325 and 3389. Fee.

Old American Campground—In the town of Newport. Campsites and boat launch. Fee.

Resorts and Businesses

Blue Slide Resort—In Blue Slide, Washington, thirty-six miles north of Newport on Highway 20. Cabins, campsites, and swimming pool.

The town of Newport offers groceries, gas, and restaurants.

Newport/Old Town Chamber of Commerce, 108 S. Washington, Newport, Wash., 99156, (509) 447-3514.

Republic Ranger District

The Republic Ranger District covers the rolling hills west of the Kettle Crest to the boundary with the Okanogan National Forest. Forests are dry, with ponderosa pine and lodgepole pine predominating.

Information Centers

Republic Ranger Station, Republic, Wash., 99166, (509) 775-3305. Staffed information desk, map and book sales, and restrooms.

Recreation Highlights

Fossil hunting—At the end of Knob Hill Road in Republic, the Stone Rose Fossil Dig offers opportunities to unearth ancient fossils. Interpretive signs and picnic tables.

Sherman Pass—Scenic views and interpretive viewpoints at the highest roaded pass in Washington—on Highway 20 between Republic and Kettle Falls.

White Mountain Fire Viewpoint—Three miles west of Sherman Pass on Highway 20. Interpretive signs tell the story of the 1988 White Mountain Fire that burned 20,000 acres of lodgepole pine and subalpine fir.

Kettle Crest Trail System—Twenty-nine miles of hiking, horse and mountain bike trails through scenic, national forest backcountry. Trail difficulties vary from easiest to most difficult. Trails cross grassy alpine meadows, talus slopes, and high peaks. Fifteen trailheads access the system, all equipped with comment boxes, water for livestock, and parking facilities.

Cross-country skiing and snowmobiling opportunities—Seventeen kilometers of machine-groomed cross-country ski trails at Boulder-Deer Creek. Backcountry touring available on the Kettle Crest Trail. State-groomed snowmobile routes at Swan Lake, Quartz Mountain, and Iron Mountain.

Campgrounds

Ferry Lake—Fourteen miles southwest of Republic via State Highway 21 and Forest Roads 53 and 800. Nine tent units, nine tent/trailer units, and drinking water. Fishing and swimming. Hiking and mountain bike trails. Elevation 3,300 feet. Fee.

Swan Lake—Fifteen miles southwest of Republic via State Highway 21 and Forest Road 53. Six picnic units, picnic shelter, four tent units, twenty-one tent/trailer units, and drinking water. Swimming and fishing. Elevation 3,700 feet. Fee.

Long Lake—Sixteen miles south of Republic via State Highway 21 and Forest Roads 53 and 400. Twelve tent/trailer units and drinking water. Swimming and fly fishing only. Elevation 3,300 feet. Fee.

Ten Mile—Ten miles south of Republic on State Highway 21. Eight campsites, no water. Restrooms.

Thirteen Mile Trailhead—Thirteen miles south of Republic on State Highway 21. Four campsites. No water. Restrooms.

Boulder/Deer Creek—Nine miles east of Curlew on Forest Road 61. Ten campsites. No water. Restrooms.

Lambert Forest Camp—Twelve miles east of Republic on Lambert Creek Road. Five campsites. Trailhead.

Resorts and Businesses

Republic has 2,000 people and offers restaurants, gas, and lodging.

Republic Chamber of Commerce, 556-3 W. Curlew Lake Rd., Republic, Wash., 99166, (509) 775-3173.

Five resorts on Curlew Lake: Triangle J, a youth hostel and a bed and breakfast.

Sullivan Lake Ranger District

The Sullivan Lake Ranger District lies in the northeast corner of the national forest in the Selkirk Mountains. The district features the many recreation opportunities around Sullivan Lake and the Salmo-Priest Wilderness Area.

Information Centers

Sullivan Lake Ranger Station, 12641 Sullivan Lake Road, Metaline, Wash., 99153, (509) 446-2681, 446-7500.

Recreation Highlights

Sullivan Lake—Natural lake raised forty feet by an artificial dam first built in 1910. The lake offers swimming, boating, fishing, waterskiing,

Hall Mountain rises above the peaceful water of Sullivan Lake. Campgrounds on the lakeshore offer boat launches and swimming. Forest Service photo.

camping, hiking, and picnicking.

Millpond Interpretive Trail—Barrier-free 0.75-mile-long trail with signs that interpret the history of a hydro-electric system that helped establish Metaline Falls. Visitors can see the remains of the beginning of a two-mile-long wooden flume six feet high and nine feet wide that carried water from a millpond to a hydro-power station in Metaline Falls. Power generated by the hydro-power station was used from 1910 to 1956 to operate a cement plant in Metaline Falls.

Noisy Creek Sheep Feeding Station—Bighorn sheep feeding station at the base of Hall Mountain near Noisy Creek Campground at the south end of Sullivan Lake. A 0.25-mile walk just off of County Road 9345. Provides close views of bighorn sheep during the winter months when they are down low to feed. During the summer the sheep graze up high, out of easy view.

Flume Creek Goat Viewing Site—Mountain goat viewing area located two miles northwest of Metaline via County Road 2975. Goats are best seen through binoculars. Best viewing times are morning or early evening on cool days in spring and fall.

Campgrounds

Millpond—Five miles northeast of Metaline Falls via State Highway 31 and County Road 9345. Ten tent/trailer units, toilets, garbage service, and drinking water. Fishing and hiking. Elevation 2,400 feet. Fee.

East Sullivan—6.5 miles northeast of Metaline Falls via State Highway 31 and County Road 9345. Four picnic sites, twenty-four tent-RV units, toilets, drinking water, trailer dump station, and garbage service. Boating, fishing, waterskiing, swimming, and picnicking. Grassy public airstrip located between East and West Sullivan campgrounds for fly-in camping. Open May through September. Elevation 2,600 feet. Fee.

West Sullivan—6.5 miles northeast of Metaline Falls via State Highway 31 and County Road 9345. Three individual and one group picnic sites; group site has covered shelter with fireplace. Ten tent/trailer units, toilets, drinking water, and garbage service. Fishing, waterskiing, swimming, and picnicking. Elevation 2,600 feet. Open all year with reduced services. Fee.

Noisy Creek—Ten miles south of Metaline Falls and thirteen miles northeast of Ione on County Road 9345. Nineteen tent/trailer units and drinking water. Fishing, hiking, boating, and swimming. Elevation 2,600 feet. Fee.

Edgewater—Located on the Pend Oreille River, two miles northeast of Ione via Highway 31 and County Roads 9345 and 3669. Five picnic sites, twenty-one tent/trailer units, toilets, boat launch, and drinking water. No garbage service. Open May through September. Elevation 2,200 feet.□

NOTES

Hikers along the Pacific Crest Trail in the Goat Rocks Wilderness can see spectacular views of cloud-capped Mount Adams to the South. Roland Emetaz photo.

GIFFORD PINCHOT NATIONAL FOREST

Volcanos created almost every square inch of land within the Gifford Pinchot National Forest. These immense, glacier-capped volcanic peaks dominate the landscape. Mount Adams and Mount St. Helens tower above the rest of the mountains within the national forest. Mount Rainier looms just north and Mount Hood rises to the south of the national forest. Between these mountains, forests grow from the surfaces of smaller volcanic cinder cones and lava flows. Lakes nestle among the lava flows, and streams and rivers flow between banks of volcanic rock.

Mount St. Helens, the active volcano that exploded on May 18, 1980, is one of the main visitor attractions within the national forest. Its blasted summit, steaming lava dome, and thousands of acres of downed trees draw millions of visitors each year from around the world. Many of the day-use recreation facilities of the national forest are clustered around the Mount St. Helens National Volcanic Monument, while overnight facilities are spread throughout the rest of the forest.

Location

The Gifford Pinchot National Forest encompasses much of the volcanic terrain of the west side of the Cascade Mountains from Mount Rainier National Park south to the Columbia River and the Oregon border.

The national forest is bordered on the north by Mount Rainier National Park and on the east by the Wenatchee National Forest and the Yakima Indian Reservation.

The nearest cities are Vancouver, Washington, and Portland, Oregon, within an hour or two of the western and southern boundaries. Tacoma and Seattle, Washington, are within an easy two-hour drive of the northern forest boundary.

Climate

Wet, mild maritime weather dominates most of the national forest during most of the year. Like other areas on the western slopes of the Cascades, the forest receives heavy rainfall and snowfall in the fall, winter, and spring and experiences a brief drought each summer.

Snowfall is heavy above 3,000 feet, and snow lies late into the summer at higher elevations. Most forest roads are closed by snow from November through April. Avalanches are common on the high, steep slopes of the volcanos during the fall, winter, and spring.

The eastern portions of the national forest, especially to the south of Mount Adams, experience some weather similar to the dry, warm conditions of eastern Washington.

Geology

The geology of the Gifford Pinchot National Forest can be summed up in two words: Volcanic eruptions! Young lava flows show up as dark tongues of rock among the trees. Some poured from craters only a few hundred years ago and look as if they cooled yesterday. Older lava flows that have resisted

GIFFORD PINCHOT NATIONAL FOREST

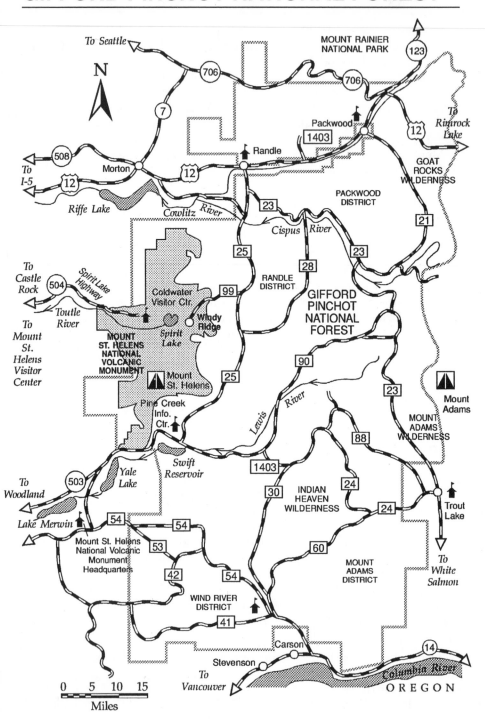

To Seattle

N

MOUNT RAINIER
NATIONAL PARK

123

706

706

To
Rimrock
Lake

Packwood

1403

12

7

Randle

GOAT
ROCKS
WILDERNESS

508

To
I-5

Morton

12

12

PACKWOOD
DISTRICT

Riffe Lake

Cowlitz River

23

21

Cispus River

25

To
Castle
Rock

504

Spirit Lake
Highway

Coldwater
Visitor Ctr.

28

23

99

RANDLE
DISTRICT

Toutle
River

Windy
Ridge

GIFFORD
PINCHOT
NATIONAL
FOREST

To
Mount
St.
Helens
Visitor
Center

MOUNT
ST. HELENS
NATIONAL
VOLCANIC
MONUMENT

Spirit
Lake

Mount
St. Helens

25

90

Lewis River

23

Mount
Adams

Pine Creek
Info.
Ctr.

MOUNT
ADAMS
WILDERNESS

88

Swift
Reservoir

1403

To
Woodland

503

Yale
Lake

30

INDIAN
HEAVEN
WILDERNESS

24

24

Trout
Lake

Lake Merwin

54

54

Mount St. Helens
National Volcanic
Monument
Headquarters

53

60

To
White
Salmon

42

54

MOUNT
ADAMS
DISTRICT

WIND RIVER
DISTRICT

41

Carson

14

Stevenson

To
Vancouver

Columbia River

OREGON

0   5   10   15

Miles

40

erosion form peaks like Tower Rock.

Ash layers underlay almost everything growing in the forest. The soil is made up of layers of ash from many different eruptions over hundreds of thousands of years. This volcanic soil helps produce some of the fastest-growing trees in the world.

The most dramatic geologic story of recent times is the 1980 eruption of Mount St. Helens, which blew more than 1,300 feet off the top of the volcano. A wave of ash, gas, and steam three times hotter than boiling water roared north at speeds faster than a jet plane can go. The ash scorched or blew down 200 square miles of trees. Fifty-seven people and countless animals lost their lives during the eruption.

The other major volcano within the national forest, Mount Adams, rises 12,276 feet to earn the title of the second highest peak in Washington. Mount Adams is really a cluster of volcanic cones ranging in age from 450,000 to 12,000 years old.

Ecology

The story of how plants and animals have responded to frequent volcanic eruptions is told and retold by the natural systems of the national forest.

Within the Mount St. Helens National Monument, natural processes are at work recolonizing the blast zone with animals and plants. Hummingbirds hover near geologists working in the steaming crater of the volcano. Pacific silver fir and mountain hemlock, buried in the snow during the eruption, survived and now seed surrounding areas. Elk graze in the weedy plants springing up among dead trees. Ten years after the 1980 eruption, almost every species that lived near Mount St. Helens before the blast had returned.

In the blast zone outside the national monument, humans are experimenting with helping nature heal its volcanic wounds. The trees downed by the blast have been harvested, producing enough wood for 150,000 houses. The land has been replanted with Douglas-fir that are thriving in the water-retaining ash. A single year's growth on some trees measures up to five feet.

Willow and cottonwood were planted along stream banks to reduce erosion, cool the water for fish, and provide cover for deer, elk, and smaller mammals. Fisheries biologists placed log sills and brush dams in creeks to create pools where sediment settles out and fish can find still-water havens. Twenty-inch trout now swim in streams that once flowed with boiling mud.

Beaver returning to the blast zone have traveled all the way up to the headwaters of streams and are again building their dams. At Meta Lake, beaver dams have raised the level of the lake so that it floods the viewing deck and interpretive signs each spring.

History

Prehistoric Indians lived in the national forest for over 10,000 years, a period during which the volcanos of the area erupted many times. An ancient ash-encased skeleton found in a farmer's field in the 1930s suggests that the Indians had reason to fear eruptions. The Klickitat and Cowlitz names for Mount St. Helens both mean "fire mountain."

After each eruption, the Indians returned to a re-shaped landscape. Some forests were destroyed, but new berry fields took their place. Some rivers were emptied of fish, but deer thrived in new open areas. As plants and animals adapted to volcanic changes, the Indians also adapted to continue to reap the bounty of this fiery place.

The history of Indians living in the national forest is well illustrated at Layser Cave in the northern part of the forest near Randle. The cave is reached by a short trail, and interpretive exhibits explain the 7,000-year history of the site.

Indians continue to live near and harvest resources from the national forest. Family groups still meet at the Indian camps in the extensive berry fields near the center of the national forest each summer to harvest berries, continuing the traditions of their ancestors.

In 1824, the British Hudson's Bay Company set up headquarters at Fort Vancouver, southwest of the national forest. The company coordinated fur trapping in most of Washington, Oregon, Idaho, and British Columbia. Fur trappers were the first non-Indians to explore what is now the national forest. Homesteaders moved into the wide valley bottoms and miners into the mountains in the late 1800s. Mining boomed during the 1890s and then died out. The timber industry geared up in the 1890s with the arrival of railroads and sawmills.

The Pacific Forest Reserve was established in 1893 and included the present national forest lands. The name changed to Mount Rainier Forest Reserve and then to the Columbia National Forest. The forest was chosen in 1949 to bear the name of the first chief of the Forest Service, Gifford Pinchot, because it was such a good example of extensive multiple use of public land. The Gifford Pinchot National Forest was known for many years as a "working forest." It produced the second largest timber cut of any national forest in the United States.

From 1933 to 1942, The Civilian Conservation Corps built trails, roads, and buildings within the national forest. Some of the best-preserved structures still are being used to house operations at the Wind River Nursery in the southern part of the forest.

Today, the national forest is much more a "recreation forest." Roads built for logging are now mostly used for scenic drives. Campgrounds bulge at the seams. Visitors come from every state in the Union and many other countries to see the results of the Mount St. Helens eruptions.

Forest-wide Recreation Opportunities

Scenic Drives

Windy Ridge—Forest Roads 25, 26, and 99 run from Randle through the 1980 blast zone to spectacular views of the Mount St. Helens crater from the south.

Spirit Lake Memorial Highway—State Highway 504 connects Interstate 5 with Coldwater Lake, offering magnificent views of the crater from the west.

Scenic drives are common in the Gifford Pinchot National Forest. Almost every forest road offers views of the grand volcanos that rise like snow cones on all sides.

Wilderness Areas

Goat Rocks Wilderness—71,670 acres within the northern part of the Gifford Pinchot National Forest. A rugged land of flinty pinnacles, glaciers, and wildflower meadows.

Mount Adams Wilderness—47,000 acres on the western slopes of Mount Adams. Trails offer spectacular views of glaciers, waterfalls, and wildflowers scattered among rubbly lava flows.

Glacier View Wilderness—3,000 acres on the western boundary of Mount Rainier National Park. Outstanding views of volcanos.

Indian Heaven Wilderness—20,600 acres of rolling hills at the crest of the Cascade Mountains. Used by local Indian tribes. Wildlife, panoramic views, wildflowers, and huckleberries.

Tatoosh Wilderness—15,800 acres on the southern boundary of Mount Rainier National Park including 550 acres of the Butter Creek Natural Area devoted to forest research.

Trapper Creek Wilderness—6,000 acres ranging from old growth Douglas-fir at low elevations to rocky peaks and high meadows.

William O. Douglas Wilderness—15,880 acres within the northeastern portion of the national forest. Named after former Supreme Court justice and local environmentalist. Scattered peaks, sharp ridges, steep slopes, and hundreds of small lakes.

Special Areas

Mount St. Helens National Volcanic Monument—110,000 acres in the western portion of the national forest. Set aside for visitors to view the results of volcanic eruptions undisturbed by human interference. A powerful eruption of Mount St. Helens in 1980 caused dramatic changes in the landscape. The monument has two visitor centers and many interpretive trails, programs, and viewpoints.

Wildlife

A wide variety of birds, mammals, and other animals lives within the national forest. The best times to observe wildlife are the early morning and late evening.

Mammals include deer, bear, grouse, mountain goat, northern pocket gopher, Pacific jumping mouse, deer mouse, golden-mantled ground squirrel, hoary marmot, pika, and elk. Birds include hairy woodpecker, common raven, mountain bluebird, white-crowned sparrow, American robin, red-breasted nuthatch, osprey, and northern flicker.

Hunting

Hunting is allowed during legal seasons for black-tailed deer, Roosevelt elk, black bear, mountain goats, and grouse. Washington State game laws apply.

Fishing

Streams harbor rainbow trout, brook trout, and cutthroat trout, and most are open for fishing during the summer months. Most high lakes melt free by late June. Lakes on Forest Service roads near campgrounds may have boat launches. Washington State fishing regulations apply.

Foraging

The berry fields of the Gifford Pinchot National Forest are famous throughout Washington. In most areas, visitors can join local Native American tribes in harvesting red and blue huckleberries, black caps, thimble berries, salmon berries, and others during the mid-summer months. A few fields are reserved for Indian use only.

Mushrooms can be gathered for home use throughout the national forest, mostly at lower elevations. Mushroom harvesters must get a permit from the Forest Service.

Firewood cutting for more than just campground use requires a permit for a fee from the Forest Service. Firewood must be taken from designated areas and must not exceed five feet in length. Wildlife trees are dead standing trees that have been preserved for habitat. Cutting such trees is prohibited.

Bear grass, or *Xerophyllum tenax*, grows in large, dense clumps of dry, stringy grass-like leaves. The plant has puffy white flowers that can be gathered to make baskets or floral arrangements.

Water Recreation

The Cispus, Lewis, and White Salmon rivers offer early season floating opportunities. Contact ranger stations for specifics.

Winter Recreation

Old Man Pass in the Upper Wind River Winter Recreation Area, Marble Mountain, White Pass, Mount Adams, and Mount St. Helens Winter Recre-

Cross-country skiers enjoy snow-covered forest roads in the winter recreation area on the south side of Mount St. Helens. Roland Emetaz.

ation Area all offer cross-country skiing, mostly on snow-covered forest roads, and snowplay areas near parking lots. Ratings of ski routes for difficulty are available from Forest Service offices.

Sno-Park permits are required for each vehicle parked in designated Sno-Park parking areas. The permits help pay for snow removal and can be purchased at local businesses or from the Washington State Parks Commission in Olympia.

White Pass Ski Area located at White Pass on U.S. Highway 12 offers downhill ski runs and groomed cross-country ski trails.

Snowmobiling is available on forest roads and on groomed trails including the Lahar and Lone Butte areas. Some routes are designated cross-country skiing only.

Avalanches can be a hazard during winter months, especially during and just after winter storms. The danger is greatest in undeveloped areas at higher elevations. Check with a Forest Service office for current avalanche conditions before attempting winter travel.

8312 Trail is an example of the fine cross-country skiing available in the forest. Its 4.5 miles of groomed trail lead to the summit of a dormant volcano, Marble Mountain. Views of snow-capped mounts Hood, Adams, Rainier, and St. Helens. Located on Forest Road 8312. Open to skiers and snowmobilers.

Off-road Vehicles and Mountain Bikes

Off-road vehicles can use forest roads and trails specifically designated for motorized vehicles.

Motor Bikes

All forest roads are open to motorbikes and several specific trails have been designated for motorized vehicles. Contact a Forest Service office for complete listings. The following is just an example.

Boundary Trail—Twenty-five miles of easy to challenging trail. Four "lift and pull" switchbacks. Motorbikes must be walked over a rocky slide. Start from Forest Road 25, 29, or 2834 near Council Lake. Great ridge riding, hillclimbs, meadows, and big trees.

Mountain Bikes

More than 500 miles of trails and 4,300 miles of roads have been designated for mountain bikes within the national forest. The wilderness areas are closed to mountain bikes. Contact a Forest Service office for a complete listing. The following is just an example of available trips.

Buck Creek Trail Loop—Begin at Buck Creek trailhead off Forest Roads 80 and 8000031 in the Mount Adams Ranger District. The loop includes forest roads 8000031, 80, 8031, 8031020, 8031050, and 8031041, and the Buck Creek Trail. The trip is about thirteen miles with eleven miles of road and three miles of trail. It usually takes about 3.5 hours. Views of Mount Adams and Mount Hood.

Backcountry Travel

More than 1,000 miles of trail access the national forest including more than 200 miles of wilderness trail. The Pacific Crest National Scenic Trail runs north/south through the forest. Trails range from flat interpretive loops of less

Mount Adams is one of the most heavily glaciated peaks in the Cascade Mountains. Climbers on the west side of the mountain encounter the Adams Glacier and the North Ridge. Roland Emetaz photo.

than a mile to much longer, more rugged trails high on the slopes of Mount Adams and Mount St. Helens.

Non-wilderness Trails

Lower Falls Creek Trail—A 1.5-mile hike to the plunge pool of a series of spectacular waterfalls that drop 250 feet. Located in the Wind River District.

Kraus Ridge—This 3.5-mile trail through old trees melts free of snow early and is open for hiking in the spring and fall and sometimes in the winter. Located in the Randle Ranger District.

Wilderness Trails

Party size limited to "twelve heart-beats" including stock and people.

Round the Mountain Trail—A fifty-mile trail leading around Mount Adams with spectacular views of Mount Adams' glaciers and ridges and surrounding mountains and valleys. The trail contours around the mountain above timberline, passing through wildflower meadows and the rocky chaos of lava flows. Part of the trail lies within the Mount Adams Wilderness and part within the Yakima Indian Reservation.

Goat Rocks Loop—A twelve-mile loop in the Goat Rocks Wilderness south of Packwood. The loop uses three trails, Snowgrass, Lily Basin, and Berry Patch. It begins seventeen miles south of Packwood via Johnston Creek Road 21 and Forest Road 2150. Wildflowers are abundant in mid-summer and views of peaks are outstanding.

Horse Trails

Wind River Valley Loop—Dry Creek Trail, Observation Trail, and Big Hollow Trail provide an enjoyable fifteen-mile loop in the southern portion of the forest.

Many other forest trails are open to stock during designated months. Check with Forest Service offices for complete listings.

Please keep stock more than 200 feet away from lakes or streams except for watering or traveling on established trail routes. Forage may be limited, so carry feed. Avoid tying horses at campsites for prolonged periods. Hobble, stake, or use picket lines. No horses are allowed within any designated campground or picnic area unless the area is specifically open to stock.

Seven horse camps are located near horse trails within the national forest. These camps offer loading ramps and tethering areas. Some have corrals. Some trailheads have loading ramps.

Mountain Climbing

Climbers ascend the dormant volcano Mount Adams, 12,276 feet, by many different routes, some relatively easy and requiring little experience, others extremely challenging and requiring extensive climbing skills. Mount Adams is really several volcanos strung together, and most of the upper reaches are glaciated. Climbers attempting Mount Adams should carry ropes, crampons, and ice axes all year.

Climbers can tackle the 8,365-foot summit of Mount St. Helens during low volcanic activity. The climb is not considered difficult by experienced climbers, but its high elevation, snow-covered slopes, and unpredictable weather can prove dangerous. Numbers are limited during the summer and permits are required all year. Climbers approach the mountain from the south, hike the Ptarmigan Trail through trees for 2.5 miles and then scramble up boulder-strewn ridges and snowfields to the rim of the crater. Those looking down from the summit can see the steaming lava dome growing within the huge crater. Average round-trip climbing time is nine to ten hours.

Barrier-free Sites

Information stations with barrier-free parking, access, and restrooms: Forest Headquarters, Vancouver, Washington, Mount St. Helens Visitor Center, Coldwater Visitor Center, and Wood's Creek Information Station which includes paved travelway to an area of identified native plants.

Campgrounds with barrier-free access to campsites and restrooms: Mount Adams District—Peterson Prairie, Moss Creek, Oklahoma, Sawtooth Berry Fields; Packwood District—La Wis Wis; Wind River District—Beaver,

Hikers on the Round-the-Mountain Trail travel around Mount Adams, passing through meadows, lava fields, and mountain lakes. Roland Emetaz photo.

Paradise, Sunset; Randle District —Takhlakh Lake (Thirty percent of camp-ground is barrier-free including one toilet).

Interpretive trails and other short trails with barrier-free sections: Mount St.Helens National Monument—Trail of Two Forests Interpretive Trail, Meta Lake Trail, Lava Canyon, Curly Creek; Wind River District—Sunset Campground, Bonneville trailhead; Randle District—Quartz Creek Big Trees (more difficult trail through 500-year-old Douglas fir and hemlock trees), Iron Creek Picnic Area, Yellow Jack Ponds.

Viewing areas with barrier-free access: Mount St. Helens National Monument—Outlaw Ridge Volcano Viewpoint, Pine Creek Information Station; Randle District—Ryan Lake, barrier-free picnic sites, restrooms, and interpretive signs.

Children's Activities

Mount St. Helens National Volcanic Monument has interpretive exhibits and programs oriented specifically for children. The monument newspaper includes a "Kids' Corner" with ideas and activities for children. Environmen-tal education curriculum materials related to Mount St. Helens are available through Forest Service offices.

Children enjoy exploring Ape Cave and the small lava tubes at Lava Cast Interpretive Trail. Guided lantern walks are scheduled during summer months. Parents should accompany children and observe safety regulations.

Forest Headquarters

Gifford Pinchot National Forest Headquarters 6926 E. Fourth Plain Blvd., P.O. Box 8944, Vancouver, WA 98668-8944, (206) 750-5000.

Ranger District Recreation Opportunities

Wind River District

The Wind River District lies in the southern part of the national forest just north of the Columbia River and between Mount Adams and Mount St. Helens.

Information Centers

Wind River Ranger Station, Carson, WA 98610-9724, (509) 427-5645. Information desk, map and book sales, and restrooms.

Recreation Highlights

Wind River Nursery—A working Forest Service nursery with historic buildings, dam, and interpretive exhibits. The nursery was established in 1909, four years after the Forest Service was created. Interpretive trail of historic arboretum. Tours are available. Nine miles north of Carson off County Road 92135 near Wind River Ranger Station.

Government Mineral Springs—Once the site of a hotel from around 1910 until 1935, when the building burned. Fifteen miles north of Carson via County Road 92135 and Forest Road 3065. Ten picnic sites, drinking water, mineral water, big trees, and hiking.

Bear Meadow Interpretive Site includes a picnic area, restrooms, interpretive signs, and great views of Mount St. Helens. Roland Emetaz photo.

Trout Creek and Hemlock Lake—Lakeside picnic area. Nine miles north of Carson off County Road 91135, near Wind River Ranger Station. Fifteen picnic units, drinking water, fishing, non-motorized boating.

Carson National Fish Hatchery—Run by the Fish and Wildlife Service, this hatchery is located near the Wind River Ranger Station. The hatchery raises salmon, rainbow trout, and brook trout for release into lakes and streams each year. Visitors are welcome. Restrooms and drinking water. Tours can be arranged.

Campgrounds

Beaver—Twelve miles northwest of Carson via County Road 92135 on Wind River. Twenty-four tent/trailer units, fourteen-unit group camp, and drinking water. Fishing and mushrooming. Elevation 1,100 feet. Fee.

Falls Creek Horse Camp—Twenty-three miles northwest of Carson via County Road 92135 and Forest Road 65. Three tent units, eight tent/trailer units, and RVs under twenty feet. Riding, hiking, berry-picking. Elevation 3,600 feet.

Panther Creek—Eleven miles north of Carson via County Road 92135 and Forest Road 65. Thirty-three tent/trailer units and drinking water. Fishing and access to the Pacific Crest Trail. Elevation 900 feet. Fee.

Paradise Creek—Twenty miles north of Carson via County Road 92135 and Forest Road 30. Forty-two tent/trailer units and drinking water. Fishing, hiking, and berry picking. Elevation 1,500 feet. Fee.

Sunset—Eleven miles east of Yacolt on County Road 12. Twenty picnic sites and ten tent/trailer units. Drinking water. Hiking, waterfall, Silver Star Mountain. Elevation 1,000 feet.

Other Campgrounds

Pacific Power, a private electric utility company, operates Cresap Bay Park and thirteen other parks and fishing access sites along the Lewis River as part of its licenses to operate three hydro-electric projects on the river.

Cresap Bay Park—Open from Memorial Day to Labor Day. Sixty campsites available on first-come, first-served basis; a group camp with covered shelter and electricity. Eighteen marina slips and barrier-free docks. Restrooms with flush toilets and showers. RV dump station but no hook-ups. Two-mile interpretive trail with brochure. Fees comparable to Washington State Parks.

Carson is a small town offering groceries, gas, and lodging. The hot springs resort near town also offers spa baths in natural mineral water.

Mount Adams Ranger District

The Mount Adams district lies in the southeastern part of the national forest and includes the volcano Mount Adams, 12,276 feet, the second highest mountain in Washington State.

Information Centers

Mount Adams Ranger Station, Trout Lake, WA 98650-9724, (509) 395-2501. Information desk, map and book sales, and restrooms.

Recreation Highlights

Lewis River—Sixteen miles northwest of Trout Lake via State Highway 141 and Forest Roads 88, 8851, and 3241.

Big Lava Bed—12,500 acres of lava beds rising from 2,000 feet in elevation at the southern end to 3,360 feet at the base of the crater. Towering rock piles, short caves, crevasses, and uniquely-shaped lava features. No known year-round water exists in Big Lava Bed, so carry water. Pay close attention to landmarks as it is easy to get lost. From Willard take forest roads 66 and 6615 to Forest Road 60.

Indian Heaven Wilderness—A roadless area eight miles in length covering 15,400 acres. Gently rolling meadows and sparse forests. Indian Heaven used to be good berry picking country, but suppression of fires has allowed trees to encroach on berry fields. Three craters are in the area: Lemei Rock, Wapiki Lake, and East Crater. Indian Race Track was used by Indians in recent history for berry picking, playing games, and horse racing. Several trails lead into Indian Heaven. Accessed via Forest Road 60, 65, 24, 30, or 6035.

Ice Cave—Lava tube cave near Ice Cave Campground. This cave served as the ice supply for the towns of Hood River and The Dalles in pioneer years. A ladder leads into the main entrance providing access to the 120-foot glacier section. Other passages continue further. Spelunkers should wear warm clothing, head protection, boots, and carry a minimum of two sources of light.

Campgrounds

Cold Springs Indian Camp—Twenty-two miles northwest of Trout Lake via State Highway 141 and Forest Road 24. Nine tent/trailer units. Lightly developed. Hiking and berry-picking. Elevation 4,200 feet.

Cultus Creek—Eighteen miles northwest of Trout Lake via State Highway 141 and Forest Road 24. Fifty-one tent/trailer units and drinking water. Hiking and berry picking. Fee. Elevation 4,000 feet.

Forlorn Lakes—Fourteen miles west of Trout Lake via State Highway 141 and Forest Roads 24, 60, and 6035. Eight tent units, RVs under sixteen feet. Fishing. Elevation 3,600 feet.

Goose Lake—Thirteen miles southwest of Trout Lake via State Highway 141 and Forest Roads 24 and 60. Twenty-four tent units, RVs under sixteen feet. Fishing and boating. Elevation 3,200 feet.

Ice Cave—Seven miles southwest of Trout Lake via State Highway 141 and Forest Road 24. Three picnic units and twelve tent/trailer units. Cave spelunking. Elevation 2,800 feet.

Little Goose—Sixteen miles northwest of Trout Lake via State Highway 141 and Forest Road 24. Eighteen tent units, ten tent/trailer units, three-unit horse camp, and drinking water. RVs to sixteen feet. Hiking and berry picking. Elevation 4,000 feet.

Meadow Creek Indian Camp—Twenty miles northwest of Trout Lake via State Highway 141 and Forest Road 24. Lightly developed. Eight tent units. Berry picking. Elevation 4,100 feet.

Morrison Creek—Twelve miles north of Trout Lake via Forest Roads 80 and 8040. Three tent units and horse camp nearby. Hiking, scenery. Elevation 4,600 feet.

Moss Creek—Eight miles north of Cook via State Highway 14 and County Road 86. Eighteen tent/trailer units and drinking water. Fee. Elevation 1,400 feet.

Oklahoma—Fourteen miles north of Cook via State Highway 14, County Road 86, and Forest Road 18. Twenty-three tent/trailer units, and drinking water. Fishing. Elevation 1,700 feet. Fee.

Peterson Prairie—Via State Highway 141 and Forest Road 24, eight miles south of Trout Lake. Thirty tent/trailer units and drinking water. Ten-unit group camp, reservations needed. Hiking and berry picking. Elevation 2,800 feet. Fee.

Saddle—Twenty-four miles northwest of Trout Lake via State Highway 141 and Forest Roads 24 and 2480. Twelve tent/trailer units. Berry picking. Elevation 4,200 feet.

South—Twenty-five miles northwest of Trout Lake via State Highway 141 and Forest Roads 24 and 2480. Nine tent/trailer units and drinking water. RVs to sixteen feet. Berry picking. Elevation 4,000 feet.

Surprise Lakes Indian Camp—Twenty-two miles northwest of Trout Lake via State Highway 141 and Forest Road 24. Lightly developed. Nine tent/trailer units. Berry picking. Elevation 4,100 feet.

Tillicum—Twenty-five miles northwest of Trout Lake via State Highway 141 and Forest Road 24. Forty-nine tent/trailer units, drinking water, and RVs to sixteen feet. Berry picking. Elevation 4,300 feet.

Smokey Creek—Twelve miles west of Trout Lake via State Highway 141 and Forest Road 24. Five tent/trailer units. Berry picking. Elevation 3,700 feet.

Resorts and Businesses

Trout Lake is a small town offering restaurants, groceries, and gas.

Packwood Ranger District

The Packwood District lies in the northeastern section of the national forest near Mount Rainier National Park and includes parts of the William O. Douglas and Goat Rocks wilderness areas.

Information Centers

Packwood Ranger Station, Packwood, WA 98361-0559, (206) 494-5515. Information desk, map and book sales, and restrooms.

Recreation Highlights

Knuppenburg—Fishing area along the highway to White Pass. Eighteen miles east of Packwood on U.S. Highway 12. Seven picnic units. Elevation 4,100 feet.

La Wis Wis—Picnic area seven miles northeast of Packwood via U.S. Highway 12. Picnic shelter and barbecue pit, twelve picnic sites.

Palisades—Geologic scenic viewpoint twelve miles northeast of Packwood via U.S. Highway 12.

Campgrounds

Big Creek—Four miles southeast of Ashford via State Highway 706 and Forest Road 52. Thirty tent/trailer units and drinking water. Fishing, hiking, near Mount Rainier National Park. Elevation 1,800 feet. Fee.

La Wis Wis—Seven miles northeast of Packwood via U.S. Highway 12 and Forest Road 1272. 101 tent/trailer units and drinking water. Fishing, hiking, and overlook. Elevation 1,400 feet. Fee.

Soda Springs—Fifteen miles northeast of Packwood via U.S. Highway 12 and Forest Roads 45 and 4510. Eight tent units. Trail access to William O. Douglas Wilderness. Elevation 3,200 feet.

Summit Lake—Fifteen miles northeast of Packwood via U.S. Highway 12 and Forest Roads 45 and 4510. Five tent units. Fishing and hiking. Elevation 2,400 feet.

Walupt Lake—Twenty-four miles southeast of Packwood via U.S. Highway 12 and Forest Roads 21 and 2160. Nine tent units, thirty-five tent/trailer units, and drinking water. Fishing, hiking, and boating. Elevation 3,900 feet. Fee.

Walupt Lake Horse Camp—Twenty-three miles southeast of Packwood via U.S. Highway 12 and Forest Roads 21 and 2160. Six tent units and drinking water. Fishing, hiking, boating, and riding. Elevation 3,900 feet.

Resorts and Businesses

The town of Packwood offers gas, groceries, lodging, and restaurants.

Randle Ranger District

The Randle District lies in the northern part of the national forest between Mount Adams and Mount St. Helens. The Cispus River drains much of the district and eventually flows into the Columbia River.

Information Centers

Randle Ranger Station, Randle WA 98377-9105, (206) 497-7565. Information desk, map and book sales, and restrooms.

Recreation Highlights

Yellow Jacket—Picnic area at stocked fishing ponds ten miles southeast of Randle via Forest Roads 23 and 76. Six picnic units. Elevation 1,100 feet.

Ryan Lake—Interpretive site related to Mount St. Helens eruptions. Reached via forest roads 25 and 26. Elevation 3,300 feet.

Layser Cave—Interpretive site at cave occupied 7,000 years ago by prehistoric Indians. Short hike off gravel road near Cispus Learning Center. Ten miles southeast of Randle. Reached via forest roads 23 and 76.

Cispus Learning Center—Located at an old Job Corps camp in the Randle Ranger District in the northern part of the national forest, this environmental education residential learning center is open all year for school and other groups. Reservations must be made ahead of time and moderate fees are charged for lodging, meals, and meeting space. Phone: (206) 497-7131.

The Cispus Learning Center near the town of Randle provides conference facilities for teacher workshops and an environmental education laboratory for public school students. Wendy Walker photo.

Campgrounds

Adams Fork—Twenty-four miles southeast of Randle via forest roads 23 and 21. Twenty-four tent/trailer units and drinking water. Fishing, hiking along Cispus River. Elevation 2,600 feet. Fee.

Blue Lake Creek—Sixteen miles southeast of Randle via forest road 23. Eleven tent/trailer units and drinking water. Fishing and hiking along Cispus River. Elevation 1,900 feet. Fee.

Cat Creek—Twenty-five miles southeast of Randle via forest roads 23 and 21. Lightly developed. Six tent units, RVs to sixteen feet. Fishing on Cispus River. Elevation 3,000 feet.

Council Lake—Thirty-five miles southeast of Randle via forest roads 23 and 2334. Six tent units and five tent/trailer units. Fishing, hiking, boating, and carry-in boat launch. Elevation 4,300 feet.

Horseshoe Lake—Forty miles southeast of Randle via forest roads 23 and 2329. Ten tent/trailer units, primitive boat launch, and RVs under sixteen feet. Fishing, hiking, and boating. Elevation 1,200 feet.

Iron Creek—Ten miles south of Randle via forest roads 23 and 25. Ninety eight tent/trailer units and drinking water. Fishing, hiking, and access to Mount St. Helens National Volcanic Monument. Elevation 1,200 feet. Fee.

Keenes Horse Camp—Thirty-nine miles southeast of Randle via forest roads 23 and 2329. Eight tent/trailer units and corral. Riding, scenery, hiking, and views of Mount Adams. Elevation 4,300 feet.

Killen Creek—Thirty-eight miles southeast of Randle via forest roads 23 and 2329. Eight tent/trailer units. Hiking, scenery, berry picking. Elevation 4,400 feet.

North Fork—Twelve miles southeast of Randle on forest road 23. Thirty-three tent/trailer units and drinking water. Group camp available by reservation for thirty people. Fishing and hiking. Elevation 1,500 feet. Fee.

Olallie Lake—Thirty-three miles southeast of Randle via forest roads 23, 2329, and 5601. Six tent/trailer units. Fishing, boating, and views of Mount Adams. Elevation 4,200 feet.

Pole Patch—Thirty-one miles south of Randle via forest roads 23, 76, and 77. Eight tent units and four tent/trailer units. Berry picking, scenery, primitive access road. Elevation 4,400 feet.

Takhlakh—Thirty-four miles southeast of Randle via forest roads 23 and 2329. Fifty-four tent/trailer units and drinking water. Views of Mount Adams, fishing, hiking, and boating. Elevation 4,500 feet. Fee.

Tower Rock—Twelve miles southeast of Randle via forest roads 23 and 76. Twenty two tent/trailer units and drinking water. Fishing. Near Cispus Learning Center. Elevation 1,100 feet. Fee.

Resorts and Businesses

Randle is a small town on U.S. Highway 12 near the national forest that offers food, groceries, lodging, and gas.

Mount St. Helens National Volcanic Monument

The Mount St. Helens National Volcanic Monument provides rare opportunities to experience an active volcano. Visitors can look into the crater and

Skiing climbers ascend the south side of Mount St. Helens by the Monitor Ridge route and then ski back down. Snow still covers most of the route until the late spring. Roland Emetaz photo.

see the steaming lava dome, view the dramatic results of the 1980 eruption of Mount St. Helens, and observe life returning to the blast zone.

The 110,000-acre national monument was created by Congress in 1982, two years after the volcano blew 1,300 feet off its summit in one cataclysmic eruption on May 18, 1980. The blast traveled 330 miles per hour and leveled 150 square miles of trees north of the volcano. Ash billowed to a height of twelve miles and spread eastward to circle the earth. The eruption transformed lush green forests into a gray moonscape.

Information Centers

Mount St. Helens National Volcanic Monument Headquarters, 42218 N.E. Yale Bridge Road, Amboy, WA 98601-9715, (206) 247-5473, TDD (206) 247-4572. Staffed information desk and map sales.

Mount St. Helens National Volcanic Monument Visitor Center, 3029 Spirit Lake Highway, Castle Rock, WA 98611. (206) 274-4038 (24-hour recording), (206) 274-6644 (office), TDD (206) 274-9344. Located five miles east of Interstate 5 on State Highway 504. Staffed information desk, map and book sales, restrooms, indoor and outdoor interpretive exhibits, interpretive programs, movies, and slide shows. Open seven days a week, all year except major holidays. Picnic and camp opportunities at nearby Seaquest State Park.

Coldwater Visitor Center—Located on Coldwater Ridge on the northwest side of Mount St. Helens via State Highway 504 east of Interstate 5. Indoor and outdoor interpretive exhibits, interpretive trail, parking, restrooms, staffed information desk, audio visual programs, interpretive presentations, and environmental education trail.

Woods Creek Information Portal—Located six miles south of Randle on Forest Road 25. Drive-up information booth, interpretive exhibits, map and book sales. Open during summer only.

Pine Creek Information Center—Near the junction of forest roads 90 and 25. Staffed information desk, map and book sales, interpretive exhibits, and videos. Open during summer only.

Apes' Headquarters—Lantern rentals, book sales, and guided interpretive cave walks. Located on forest road 8303. Open seven days a week during summer months.

Recreation Highlights

Windy Ridge—Scenic viewpoint with spectacular vistas of Mount St. Helens and the lava dome growing inside the crater. Interpretive exhibits, live programs. Interpretive trail and hiking trails. Accessed from the north via Highway 12 and the town of Randle and forest roads 25, 26, and 99, and from the south via forest road 90, the town of Cougar, and forest roads 25, and 99. Summer access only.

Spirit Lake Memorial Highway—State Highway 504 running from Interstate 5 to the Coldwater Visitor Center, Coldwater Lake (open 1993 or 1994), and on to Johnston Ridge (open 1995 or later). Two-lane paved highway with turnouts offering interpretive viewpoints. Visitor center, interpretive trails, programs, exhibits, and magnificent views of Mount St. Helens.

Ape Cave—A 12,810 foot-long lava tube formed by a basalt flow from Mount St. Helens in A.D. 40. The longest intact tube in the continental United States. Open for spelunking. Food, beverages, and rock collecting prohibited in order to protect the fragile cave environment. Take flashlight or lantern and wear warm clothes and sturdy shoes. Hard hats are recommended. Located nine miles northeast of Cougar via State Highway 503 and forest roads 90, 83, and 8303. Hiking and volcano viewing. Elevation 2,100 feet.

Trail of Two Forests—Interpretive boardwalk trail beside molds of trees made in a lava flow. Located nine miles northeast of Cougar via State Highway 503 and forest roads 90, 83, and 8303. Hiking. Elevation 1,800 feet. Barrier-free trail.

Bear Meadow—Volcano viewpoint, picnic facilities, restrooms, and interpretive exhibits. Located forty-four miles northeast of Cougar via State Highway 503 and Forest Roads 90, 25, and 99. Accessed from the north via forest roads 25 and 99 from Randle.

Meta Lake/Miner's Car—Located at the junction of forest roads 26 and 99. Interpretive sign at the rusted remains of a car caught in the 1980 eruption. Short trail from the car to the Meta Lake trail, which is a 0.2-mile easy walk into Meta Lake on a barrier-free, paved trail. Trail wanders through fallen trees; an observation deck at the lake has interpretive signs. Good foggy day hike.

Norway Pass—Norway Pass trailhead located off Forest Road 26 one mile from the intersection with Forest Road 99. Parking, restrooms, information board, and hiking trail. The Boundary Trail from Bear Meadow crosses the road here. Hikers heading west for Norway Pass can hike 2.2 miles to the pass. Classic views of Mount St. Helens from north across Spirit Lake.

Independence Pass—Trailhead to pass located on Forest Road 99. Walk 0.5 mile up switchbacks to ridgetop and Independence Pass to see Spirit Lake and Mount St. Helens. Continue on trail for a couple of miles to outstanding crater viewpoint. Continue for a total of 3.5 miles to Norway Pass.

Quartz Creek Big Trees—Accessed from Randle on forest roads 25 and 26. Turn off on Forest Road 2608 and drive one mile. Barrier-free 0.25-mile interpretive trail through a grove of ancient Douglas fir trees.

Cedar Creek Vista—Road turnout along Forest Road 99. Views of upper end of Spirit Lake. Interpretive sign.

Muddy River Viewpoint—Road turnout on Forest Road 25 near Cedar Flats. Views of the effects of volcanic mudflows. Interpretive sign.

Lahar Viewpoint—On the south side of Mount St. Helens on Road 83 near Ape Cave. Drive eleven miles up Road 83 after the turnoff from Road 90. The closest view of the mountain from the south side. Interpretive signs, trails, picnic area, restrooms, and access to lava canyon. Mudflow scoured out trees and soil in canyon, exposing rock formations such as basalt columns. Barrier-free trail for one mile to viewpoint.

Coldwater Lake (open 1993 or 1994)—Located just beyond the Coldwater Visitor Center via Spirit Lake Memorial Highway. Boat launch, picnic area, boardwalk trail along lakeshore, interpretive signs, and the Hummocks Interpretive Trail, with the first section barrier-free.

Campgrounds

Lower Falls—Thirty miles northeast of Cougar via State Highway 503 and Forest Road 90. Twenty tent/trailer units. Hiking and fishing on North Fork of the Lewis River. Elevation 1,610 feet.

Iron Creek—Ten miles south of Randle via forest roads 23 and 25. Ninety-eight tent/trailer units and drinking water. Fishing, hiking, and access to Mount St. Helens Volcanic Monument. Elevation 1,200 feet. Fee.

Other campgrounds

Pacific Power, a private electric utility company, operates Cresap Bay Park and thirteen other parks and fishing access sites along the Lewis River as part of its licenses to operate three hydro-electric projects on the river.

Cresap Bay Park—Open from Memorial Day to Labor Day. Sixty campsites available on first-come, first-served basis, a group camp with covered shelter and electricity. Eighteen marina slips and barrier-free docks. Restrooms with flush toilets and showers. RV dump station but no hook-ups. Two-mile interpretive trail with brochure. Fees comparable to Washington State Parks.

Ike Kinswa State Park—North of Highway 12 on Mayfield Lake. Sixty campsites and forty-one sites with hook-ups, barrier-free access, boat launch, trailer dump. Reservations during summer. Fee. Phone: (206) 983-3402.

Lewis and Clark State Park—Twelve miles northeast of Chehalis. Twenty-five campsites, group site. Fee. Phone: (206) 864-2643.

Paradise Point State Park—Five miles south of Woodland. Seventy campsites, boat launch, trailer dump. Fee. Phone: (206) 263-2350.

Seaquest State Park—Five miles east of Castle Rock. Seventy-four campsites, sixteen sites with hook-ups, group site, barrier-free access, trailer dump. Fee. Phone: (206) 274-8633.

Resorts and Businesses

Cougar and Amboy are small towns located near the monument that offer gas, groceries, restaurants, and lodging.

There is a small grocery store located near Pine Creek Information Station.

Crater House concession, located along Forest Road 99 on the way to Windy Ridge, offers a small restaurant, restrooms, and gift shop.□

A mountain biker enjoys a back road in the national forest. Curtis Edwards photo.

IDAHO PANHANDLE NATIONAL FORESTS

Washington, Idaho, and Montana share the rocky crags, huckleberry fields, and thick forests of the Idaho Panhandle National Forests. In Washington State, the wet, mild climate and rich soils of the west slopes of the Selkirk Mountains support thriving forests and abundant wildlife.

The 125,000 acres of Idaho Panhandle National Forests in Washington are tucked away from population centers, so the area remains relatively uncrowded and undeveloped. Part of the Washington portion of the national forest lies within the Salmo-Priest Wilderness.

Location
The Idaho Panhandle National Forests include a small part of northeastern Washington along the border between Washington and Idaho. The area used to be part of the old Kaniksu National Forest and the Kaniksu name still shows up on older maps. The Washington part of the national forest is bounded on the north, west, and south by the Colville National Forest and on the east by the Idaho border.

The nearest large cities are Spokane, Washington, and Coeur d'Alene, Idaho. Smaller towns nearby include Newport, Washington, Priest River, Idaho, and Sandpoint, Idaho. Visitors reach the Washington part of the national forest by driving Highway 2 from the west or east to Priest River, Idaho and then taking Highway 57 north. Forest roads then branch off into the national forest.

Climate
The western slopes of the Selkirk Mountains have a maritime climate similar to the western Cascades further to the west in Washington. Summer temperatures vary from sixty to ninety degrees. Winters are wet with temperatures varying from below zero to forty degrees. Average rainfall near Priest Lake is thirty-three inches a year. Snow depths vary from three to five feet in the lower areas and average ten feet in the mountains.

Geology
The northern section of the mountains of northeastern Washington were heavily glaciated many times during the last two million years of ice ages. The glaciers ground off the lower mountains into rounded humps. The peaks above the ice were sculpted into sharp pinnacles and ridges. As the glaciers retreated around 10,000 years ago, they created shallow lakes by leaving behind ice chunks the size of city blocks. These stranded icebergs melted and the remaining holes filled with water.

Much of the soil in the national forest consists of volcanic ash deposited from eruptions of Cascade Mountain volcanos over the last one million years. Most of the ash came from the explosive eruption of Mount Mazama 6,700 years ago. This eruption blew the top off of Mount Mazama to form Crater Lake in Oregon. The volcanic soil has a high nutrient and water-holding

IDAHO PANHANDLE NATIONAL FORESTS

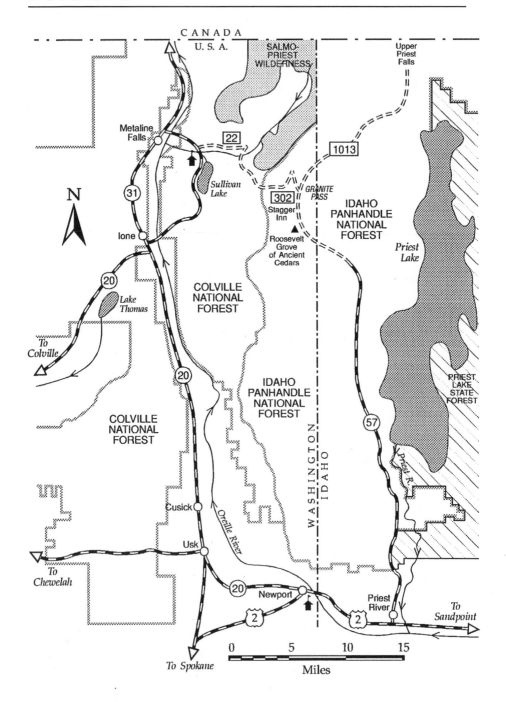

CANADA
U. S. A.

SALMO-PRIEST WILDERNESS

Upper Priest Falls

Metaline Falls

22

1013

31

Sullivan Lake

GRANITE PASS

302

Stagger Inn

IDAHO PANHANDLE NATIONAL FOREST

Ione

Roosevelt Grove of Ancient Cedars

Priest Lake

N

20

Lake Thomas

COLVILLE NATIONAL FOREST

To Colville

20

IDAHO PANHANDLE NATIONAL FOREST

PRIEST LAKE STATE FOREST

57

Priest R.

COLVILLE NATIONAL FOREST

WASHINGTON

IDAHO

Cusick

Oreille River

Usk

To Chewelah

20

Newport

2

Priest River

2

To Sandpoint

To Spokane

0   5   10   15

Miles

capacity and helps account for the lush forests of the area.

The Selkirks are foothills of the Rocky Mountains, made of sedimentary layers of sand and silt laid down in a shallow sea, starting around 1,500 million years ago and continuing for 600 million years. Tens of thousands of feet of sedimentary layers eventually accumulated and solidified into sedimentary rocks such as siltites and quartzites.

About ninety million years ago, magma surged upward into the sediments, cooling under the surface to form a huge mass of granite called the Kaniksu Batholith. The entire region was then uplifted, folded, and faulted a number of times. Finally, erosion stripped away overlying rocks, exposing some of the granite at the surface.

Ecology

The forests of the western Selkirks grow western hemlock, western white pine, Douglas-fir, western larch, and western red cedar trees. Groundcover plants such as queenscup, trillium, and lady fern grow among the trees. Wild ginger adds a pungent smell to the air. Red squirrels chatter and varied thrush trill from the tree branches.

Boggy lakes grow several species of sensitive plants. Bog cranberries ripen each summer. Some lakes even host carnivorous plants. Sundews with their small round leaves look innocent, but when insects land on their sticky leaves, long hairs slowly bend in to trap their prey. Then the sundews digest the insects through the leaves.

Fires have swept the national forest many times. Between 1900 and 1930, more than fifty percent of the national forest burned. Groves of trees like the Roosevelt Grove of Ancient Cedars escaped the flames because they were rooted in wet areas near creeks.

History

The Selkirk Mountains were the seasonal home, grocery store, workplace, and church for many tribes of prehistoric Indians. Kutenai and Kalispel Indians still gather resources in the forest today.

Fur traders, miners, loggers, and ranchers moved into the area during the 1800s, displacing the Indians to reservations. Homesteaders claimed the fertile lowlands for farming. The federal lands became national forests in 1905 and have been managed since by the Forest Service.

The Stagger Inn Campground was once a fire camp during the forest fires of 1926. Legend has it that fire fighters who had to hike the fifteen miles from the town of Nordman could only "stagger in" when they reached camp.

Forest-wide Recreation Opportunities

Scenic Drives

Pass Creek Pass, connecting Nordman, Idaho, with Metaline Falls, Washington. forest roads 302 and 22. Scenic views of Selkirk Mountains. Narrow, gravel road, not suitable for trailers.

Wilderness Areas

Salmo-Priest Wilderness—9,940 acres of the wilderness lie within the national forest, offering scenic views of the Selkirk Mountains. The wilderness offers habitat for caribou and grizzly bear and secluded hiking and wilderness serenity for human visitors.

Wildlife

A few remaining grizzly bear and wolves roam the Idaho Panhandle National Forests. The secretive grizzlies inhabit the dense forests and open brush fields common throughout the Selkirk Mountains. The mountainous area is also home to the last remaining herd of woodland caribou in the continental United States.

The caribou and wolves are listed as endangered species by the U.S. Fish and Wildlife Service, while the grizzly is listed as a threatened species. The national forest is cooperating with British Columbia, Washington, and Idaho to develop recovery plans for these rare animals.

Areas with minimal road access are set aside for the grizzly to maintain the privacy the big bears require, but no new bears are brought to the area. The caribou herd is being enlarged with animals imported from Canada.

Hunting

Hunters stalk deer and elk each fall. Special seasons in some areas allow bow hunters and muzzleloader hunters to practice their pioneer skills. The national forest also is one of the only areas in Washington where hunters get a once-in-a-lifetime chance to bag a moose.

Fishing

Streams flowing into Priest Lake are generally closed to fishing to protect spawning cutthroat and bull trout. Small lakes such as Muskegon and Petit are open and stocked on a regular basis.

Foraging

Huckleberries grow thickly in the national forest, luring many recreational pickers to harvest them every year. Especially good berry fields can be found east of Newport.

Mushrooms, other forest edibles, and firewood are also available for home use. Permits are required for commercial gathering.

Winter Sports

Cross-country Skiing

Mountain Meadows Guest Ranch, with miles of marked trails within the national forest, is located near the lower West Branch of the Priest River. Access by Forest Road 308.

Snowmobiling

Thirty miles of marked and groomed trails are located in the South Baldy and Pyramid Pass areas. Trails are accessed by the Pend Oreille River Road, Forest Road 305. Granite Falls is also a popular winter destination.

Off-road Vehicles and Mountain Bikes

Forest roads are open for motorized and wheeled bikes and 4 x 4 vehicles unless they are closed with gates to protect grizzly or caribou habitat. Vehicles must be street-legal and drivers must be licensed. Most trails are within the wilderness area and are closed to motorized and wheeled vehicles.

Backcountry Travel

Sixty miles of trails access the Washington portion of the Idaho Panhandle National Forests, most within the Salmo-Priest Wilderness. A complete listing of trails is available from the Priest Lake Ranger Station. The following hikes are examples of possible trips.

Roosevelt Trail—Trailhead located near Stagger Inn Campground on Forest Road 302. Switchbacks climb 4.5 miles to a grove of big western redcedar. This grove is above Roosevelt Grove near the campground. Other trails lead to Little Grass Mountain, Boulder Mountain, and Zero Creek.

Grassy Top Trail—Trailhead located 3.5 miles south of the Stagger Inn entrance. A challenging eight-mile hike to Grassy Top Mountain.

Barrier-free Sites

Forest information stations and some restrooms offer barrier-free access, including the restrooms at Lower Roosevelt Grove.

Children's Activities

Children enjoy the trail from Stagger Inn Campground to Granite Falls and the Roosevelt Grove of Ancient Cedars. The falls is intriguing with its

Granite Falls slices sideways through granite rocks near Roosevelt Grove of Ancient Cedars. A short hiking trail climbs alongside the falls, offering scenic viewpoints of the falls and huge old cedar trees. Forest Service photo.

sideways motion and the big trees are awe-inspiring.

Visits to the lookouts within the national forest, such as Indian Mountain and South Baldy, can be fun for kids. They enjoy climbing the stairs, seeing the living quarters, and talking to the person staffing the lookout.

Forest Headquarters

Idaho Panhandle National Forest Headquarters, 1201 Ironwood, Coeur d'Alene, Idaho 83814, (208) 765-7223.

Ranger District Recreation Opportunities

Priest Lake Ranger District

The ranger district includes the territory to the west of Priest Lake, including the section in Washington State.

Information Centers

Priest Lake Ranger Station, HCR 5, Box 207, Priest River, Idaho 83856, (208) 443-2512.

Staffed information desk, map and book sales, and restrooms.

Recreation Highlights

Roosevelt Grove of Ancient Cedars—A grove of western redcedar trees more than 1,000 years old. Some trees are seven feet in diameter. A nature trail less than a mile long passes through the upper and lower groves and goes on to overlooks of Granite Falls. Located near Stagger Inn Campground eleven miles north of Nordman, Idaho, on Forest Road 302.

Granite Falls—Spectacular sloping falls that gushes over solid granite. An overlook trail travels above the falls for dramatic views over a sheer cliff. Adjacent to Stagger Inn Campground and Roosevelt Grove of Ancient Cedars.

Priest Lake Museum and Visitor Center—Information and displays about Priest Lake, Idaho, and the national forest. Local history, geology, and forest management exhibits. Located at Luby Bay, just north of Hills Resort, adjacent to Priest Lake.

Lookouts—Two fire lookouts with spectacular views are staffed in the summer and welcome visitors. Indian Mountain, located off the Nordman-Metaline Road and South Baldy, off the Kings Lake Road.

Campgrounds

Stagger Inn—Twelve miles north of Nordman on Forest Road 302. Four tent sites. Hiking, Granite Falls and Roosevelt Grove of Ancient Cedars. (note: the Forest Service plans to convert this campground to a day-use area only. Check the campground status at the Priest Lake Ranger Station before traveling to the site.)

Dispersed Camping

Campsites at Petit Lake, Forest Road 311, and Muskegon Lake, Forest Road 1013. Camping is allowed in most areas of the national forest unless specifically prohibited. Campers must carry a shovel and bucket for fire control and make sure campfires are out when leaving.

Small streams throughout the national forest provide habitat for fish and other aquatic organisms. Forest Service photo.

The Priest Lake Ranger District has many other campgrounds, many offering lakeside camping and water sports. Contact the ranger district for further information.

Resorts and Businesses

The town of Priest Lake, Idaho, offers a full range of services including gas, groceries, restaurants, and lodging.☐

Mild temperatures and heavy rainfall in the Olympic National Forest help grow some of the most lush forests in the world. Mike Wewar photo.

OLYMPIC NATIONAL FOREST

The Olympic Mountains swell up like a dome in the middle of the Olympic Peninsula. Glaciers cap and carve the peaks in the center. Rivers run down all sides in a radiating pattern of valleys. Some of the biggest trees in the world grow on the Olympic Peninsula, 600-pound elk roam the forests, and salmon teem in the clear, cold rivers.

Olympic National Forest is isolated from urban areas by water and mountains. Its rustic campgrounds, lakes, saltwater beaches, quiet trails, breathtaking vistas, rugged peaks, and roaring rivers offer a peaceful escape from the stress of modern life.

Location

The Olympic National Forest runs around the waist of the Olympic Mountains at the western edge of Washington State. Most of the national forest's 632,324 acres lie on timbered ridges and in valleys from 500 to 3,500 feet above sea level. The peaks and meadows of Olympic National Park rise above the national forest. Indian reservations, state forests, and private lands spread over the lowlands below it.

Seattle and Tacoma, the closest large cities, are within fifty miles of the eastern part of the national forest. The smaller city of Olympia, the state capital, lies to the south. The salt water of Puget Sound lies between the cities and the forest. The Hood Canal Bridge and Washington State ferries transport cars across the sound. Highway 101 circles the Olympic Peninsula, providing access to the extensive system of gravel roads that enter the national forest.

Climate

The climate within the national forest varies from wet, mild maritime conditions on the western side to much drier weather on the eastern side. A scenic drive on Highway 101 from the west slopes of the Olympic Mountains near Lake Quinault to the east slopes near Hood Canal takes travelers from rain forests that receive some of the heaviest precipitation in the world to drier forests that resemble parts of arid eastern Washington. The rainshadow of the mountains causes the differences in rainfall.

Geology

Volcanic rocks dominate Olympic Peninsula geology. Most roadcuts expose greenish-black rock faces of eroded basalt. These rocks were once molten and erupted as lava from ancient volcanos. Geologists think that the Olympic Mountains resulted from a crumpling of the edge of North America as the Pacific Ocean floor slid beneath the continent. Volcanos then erupted through cracks in the crumpled continental rocks. Extensive ice-age glaciers carved away the top layers of volcanic rock to expose the roots of the volcanos. Alpine glaciers remain active today at the highest elevations of the Olympic Mountains, especially on the highest peak, Mount Olympus.

Ecology

Vegetation varies within the national forest, from wet forests of Sitka

OLYMPIC NATIONAL FOREST

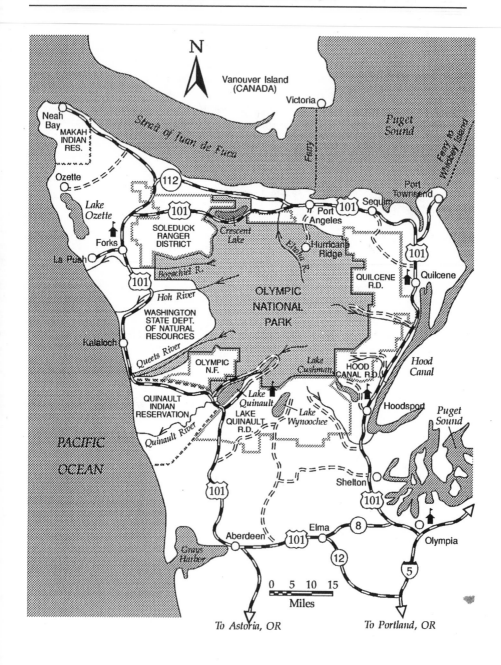

spruce and sword fern near the Pacific Ocean to dry isolated stands of lodgepole pine near the eastern extremes of the national forest. Douglas fir and western hemlock are found between the extremes. World-record sizes for several species of trees are found on the Olympic Peninsula. For example, the world's largest Sitka spruce can be seen in a private campground along the southern shores of Lake Quinault in the western portion of the national forest.

The lush forests of the western part of the national forest have been called the only temperate rain forest in the world. They are not true rain forests, however, because they experience very little rainfall each July and August. Trees that need constant moisture such as Sitka spruce survive the summer drought because fog blows in off the Pacific Ocean and drenches them on most days. These summer fogs add as much as four feet of moisture to yearly precipitation.

Rare plant communities grow within some wilderness areas high in the mountains in places such as the Buckhorn Mountain area. These plants are remnants of the last ice-age when some high peaks and ridges remained ice-free and provided refuges for organisms to escape the glaciers. When the ice melted away, the isolated plant communities were surrounded by very different post-ice-age plant associations.

History

Indians migrated to the Olympic Peninsula after the ice retreated from the last ice-age around 13,000 years ago. Their presence is marked by archaeological sites such as the shell midden near Seal Rock Campground on the eastern side of the national forest. Around 800 years ago, Indians fished for salmon, harpooned seals, dug clams, and picked oysters along the beaches of Hood Canal. They piled the empty shells from their meals in garbage heaps that remain today. These shell middens contain animal bones and discarded tools, providing valuable clues to how the people lived.

A museum at Neah Bay at the northwestern tip of the peninsula offers exhibits that chronicle how the Makah tribe lived by whaling. Native Americans still live on the Olympic Peninsula and substantial portions of the land lie within reservations such as the Quinault Reservation to the west of the national forest on the Pacific Ocean. The tribes control access to reservation lands and retain treaty rights to natural resources such as salmon.

Except for landfalls by a few early ocean explorers, non-Indian pioneers first came to the Olympic Peninsula in the 1800s, looking for mining claims, timber, and homesteads. The dense forests and steep mountains of the Olympic Mountains discouraged intense settlements. The area remains relatively undeveloped and isolated today.

The Civilian Conservation Corps was active within the Olympic National Forest during the 1930s. This federal government work program built trails, fire towers, and guard stations. A lovely example of their craftsmanship, the Hamma Guard Station, still overlooks the Hamma River Valley on the eastern side of the forest. The nearby Interorrem Guard Station was built by the Forest Service in 1907, two years after the creation of the agency.

Logging companies built their own company towns while logging in isolated areas of the national forest in the 1940s and 1950s. Camp Grisdale, in the southern part of the national forest near Wynoochee Lake, was established in 1946 and boasted bunkhouses, water tanks, family homes, a school, and a baseball team. With the improved transportation offered by modern roads, the logging camps were torn down.

Forest-wide Recreation Opportunities

Scenic Drives

Highway 101 circles the Olympic Peninsula for 340 miles and offers views into the Olympic National Forest and Olympic Mountains. Forest roads branching off the highway provide 2,500 miles of scenic driving on one-lane gravel roads.

The Quinault Valley Loop Auto Tour is a twenty-five mile paved and gravel loop extending around Lake Quinault on the western side of the national forest just off Highway 101. This 1.5-hour drive provides views of Lake Quinault, Quinault River, Colonel Bob Wilderness, rain forest, and Roosevelt elk.

Mount Walker is the only peak facing Puget Sound with road access to the top. The drive to the Mount Walker Observation Area begins five miles south of Quilcene on Highway 101. Forest Road 2730 takes visitors to viewpoints at Mount Walker's summit, 2,804 feet above sea level. The road is narrow, steep, and gravel with turnouts. It is not recommended for trailers or motorhomes.

Wilderness Areas

The wilderness areas in Olympic National Forest are located in high elevation areas including ridges and mountaintops. Trails are usually steep and scenery spectacular.

The Buckhorn Wilderness—44,258 acres on the east side of the national forest, features a wide variety of vegetation. Trail access is via forest roads off Highway 101 near Hood Canal.

The Brothers Wilderness—includes 16,412 acres of steep, forested slopes on the east side of the national forest. Trail access is via forest roads off Highway 101 near Hood Canal.

The Mount Skokomish Wilderness—encompasses 13,015 acres of rugged terrain on the southeast side of the national forest. Trail access is via forest roads off Highway 101 near Hood Canal.

The Colonel Bob Wilderness—offers 11,961 acres on the west side of the national forest near Lake Quinault. Trail access is via forest roads off Highway 101 near Lake Quinault.

The Wonder Mountain Wilderness—preserves 2,349 acres near Lake Cushman on the south side of the national forest. Trail access is forest roads off Highway 101 near Hood Canal.

Wildlife

The Olympic National Forest provides habitat for sixty-one species of mammals, 226 species of birds, seven species of reptiles, and fifteen species of amphibians. More than 3,000 Roosevelt elk roam the western side of the mountains. Some species, such as Olympic marmot and Cope's salamander,

Scenic vistas await travelers around every turn along the 2,500 miles of gravel forest roads in the Olympic National Forest. Mike Wewar photo.

are native only to the Olympics. Wildlife can be viewed along scenic drives, while hiking the trails, or during boat and raft trips.

Migratory birds found within the national forest include whistling swan, snow goose, Canada goose, common snipe, mallard duck, wood duck, harlequin duck, and common merganser. Resident birds include ring-necked pheasant, quail, golden eagle, bald eagle, common loon, gray jay, Steller's jay, mountain bluebird, cedar waxwing, raven, crow, varied thrush, and many others. Bird watching opportunities abound in the national forest, especially near lakes, rivers, and the ocean.

Hunting

Hunters stalk Columbian black-tailed deer, bear, grouse, mountain goat, and Roosevelt elk each year during hunting season. The elk can reach up to 600 pounds and are a major hunting and wildlife-watching attraction. Washington State Department of Wildlife regulates the hunts and hunting licenses are mandatory. Animals protected from hunting include: fisher, yellow pine chipmunk, hoary marmot, Douglas squirrel, Pacific green turtle, spotted owl, and northern flying squirrel. Prime hunting areas include clearcuts where wildlife feed on new growth.

Fishing

Salmon thrive in the clear, cold rivers of the Olympic Peninsula and are the livelihood for a wide variety of anglers including humans and black bear. Salmon that have been feeding in the Pacific Ocean for several years return to spawn in the tributary creeks of the rivers and then die. The rotting carcasses then recycle nutrients back into the forest. Salmon can be seen spawning in shallow water in streams and rivers during the late summer and fall. Shellfish along Hood Canal include: oysters, geoduck, crab, and steamer clams. Marine mammals such as seals can sometimes be viewed from Seal Rock Campground.

Shellfish harvesting and fishing are regulated by the Washington Department of Fisheries and the Quinault Indian Tribe at Lake Quinault. Tribal and state licenses can be purchased at local businesses. State fishing licenses are required within Olympic National Forest, but no license is required to fish in Olympic National Park. Fishing season begins in April and extends into October. High lakes often stay frozen until mid-June.

Foraging

Berry-picking season begins in July and extends through September. Huckleberries, red and blue varieties, are found in the low, wet forests and subalpine slopes. Berries ripen first at lower elevations. They are found on open forest land, cutover timberlands, and burned areas. Huckleberries are good eaten fresh and excellent in pies, jams, and jellies.

Blackberries begin to ripen in June. Common in wooded areas, along roads, fences, railroad tracks, in vacant lots, and cutover forests by the sides of streams. Excellent when eaten fresh or in pies or jams.

Red and blue elderberries are common, but only the blue should be eaten. Blue elderberries ripen from late July through September. Found along roads and in cutover areas.

Salal berries are abundant, easy to pick, and often ignored. Ripen from mid-July to mid-September. Ideal for jellies. Look for them everywhere in wooded areas.

Oregon grape should not be eaten fresh because of laxative effect. Good mixed with other berries in jellies.

Wild strawberries are found along roads or in open areas. Small, sweet berries. Good for fresh eating and in all berry baked goods.

Blackcaps are found in open or burned areas. Excellent fresh or cooked.

The wet lowland forests of the Olympic National Forest are ideal for growing mushrooms. The national forest offers excellent mushroom-picking opportunities along forest roads and trails. Morel mushrooms grow during the spring, while the other mushrooms such as chanterelles and boletes are more common in the late summer and fall. Mushroom pickers should be very careful to check species characteristics as poisonous mushrooms also grow within the national forest. Mushroom guides are sold in many forest information stations.

Water Sports

The lakes of the national forest offer boating and swimming. Rivers offer opportunities for canoeing, kayaking, and rafting. Some lakeside resorts on larger lakes, such as Lake Quinault, rent boats. Most bodies of water within the national forest are very cold all year. Boaters should wear life vests at all times.

The national forest is bordered on three sides by salt water and blessed with numerous freshwater lakes, including Lake Quinault to the west, Lake Cushman to the east, and Wynoochee Reservoir on the southern part of the national forest. Small glacier-created tarns glisten on the mountain ridges in the wilderness areas.

Winter Sports

Cross-country skiing, snowshoeing, and snowmobiling are popular on over two thousand miles of forest roads. The lowest elevation roads stay snow-free for most of the winter, but higher elevations are snow-covered from November through April. No commercial ski areas operate within the Olympic National Forest. A rope tow is open to visitors at Hurricane Ridge in Olympic National Park near Port Angeles.

Winter recreationists in the backcountry should be aware of and prepared for avalanche danger and hypothermia. Extra clothing, food, winter outer-wear, the ten essentials for backcountry travel, and informing someone of the party's whereabouts can ensure a safe return.

Mountain Bikes

Mountain bikers can find thirty bike trails totaling eighty-five miles. Only trails specifically signed as bike trails are open to mountain bikes. Wheeled vehicles are not allowed within wilderness areas. A good bike trip on the east side of the national forest includes the 6.2 miles of the Lower Quilcene Trail and connected forest roads to create a loop eighteen miles long.

Off-road Vehicles

Motorcyclists and four-wheel-drive enthusiasts can enjoy the challenging scenic forest roads. Vehicles must be street-legal and drivers must be licensed.

Backcountry Travel

Trails in the Olympic National Forest vary from relatively level walks along forested valleys to very steep rigorous climbs up mountain slopes. Trailhead signs indicate whether the trail is open to stock, motorized vehicles, or mountain bikes, as well as hikers. Wilderness trails are closed to wheeled and motorized vehicles including mountain bikes.

The 200 miles of trail within the national forest provide access to secluded camp spots, scenic viewpoints, lakes, streams, and wilderness areas. Several short trails offer interpretive exhibits such as the Shell Midden Trail near Seal Rock Campground. Many national forest trails connect with the Olympic National Park trail system.

Backcountry use rules vary between the national park and the national forest. For instance, within the national park, hikers must camp at designated campsites, while within the national forest any area is open for camping unless designated otherwise. Pets are allowed on national forest trails but not on trails in the national park.

Special rules also apply within wilderness areas. For instance, party size cannot exceed twelve people. Contact an information station for the regulations for each hiking area.

Other guides and maps provide extensive information about hiking in the national forest and are available at forest service information stations. The following are just a sampler of available opportunities.

Non-wilderness Trails

Lake Quinault Rain Forest Nature Trail: Lake Quinault on the west side of the national forest. An easy 0.5-mile trail that takes forty-five minutes. It offers interpretive signs on rain forest features. The trail follows a narrow gorge cut by a cascading stream. The route travels through towering trees, and a bog. Hikers can continue along the Quinault Loop Trail for four miles. Allow two to three hours for the longer hike.

Mount Zion Trail: trailhead located thirteen miles northwest of Quilcene on Forest Road 2810. This 1.8-mile trail ascends through new-growth forest to a picnic and camping area on top. Great views of Puget Sound, Mount Baker, Mount Rainier, and the Cascades. Motorized vehicles, mountain bikes, and stock are permitted.

Wilderness Trails

Colonel Bob Trail: this steep, strenuous trail provides access to the Colonel Bob Wilderness on ridges just south of Lake Quinault on the west side of the national forest. The trail climbs about 1,400 feet with a round trip of 14.5 miles. The trailhead is located 3.8 miles east of the ranger station at Lake Quinault.

Mildred Lakes Trail: this strenuous ten-mile round-trip trail provides access to the Mount Skokomish Wilderness on the east side of the national forest. The trail is primitive and has extremely steep pitches. The elevation gain is 2,220 feet. The lakes offer cutthroat trout, huckleberries, and mosquitoes. Trailhead is located on Forest Road 25 off Highway 101.

Mountain Climbing

The higher peaks in the Olympic Mountains tend to be within the Olympic National Park rather than in the national forest. Often the climbing access routes pass through the national forest. The rugged peaks along the east side of the national forest are popular climbing challenges. These mountains lie close to Seattle and Tacoma, so they attract urban climbers.

Climbers in the Olympics should be prepared for almost any weather and for quick changes in weather. Each member of the party should carry warm clothes, rain gear, and the ten essentials, and any groups traveling on snow or ice should carry ice axes and ropes. Rock climbers should be especially wary of rotten rock. Climbing registers are available at most information stations. Detailed climbing guides including routes and specific access directions are available at Forest Service information stations.

Barrier-free Sites

Visitor information stations provide barrier-free access to exhibits, sales, bathrooms, and information desks. Most campgrounds have barrier-free sites and restrooms.

Children's Activities

U.S Forest Service interpretive programs are offered at Lake Quinault Lodge during the summer. Many of these programs are oriented toward families and children.

Children enjoy the gravel beaches at Lake Quinault and Wynoochee Reservoir for swimming and beach play. Even young children can walk the easy Lake Quinault Rain Forest Nature Trail and marvel at features like bald eagle nests and huge old trees.

Forest Headquarters Olympic National Forest Headquarters, 1835 Black Lake Blvd. SW Olympia, WA 98502, (206) 956-2400.

Ranger District Recreation Opportunities

Hood Canal Ranger District

Information Centers

Hood Canal Ranger Station, P.O. Box 68, Hoodsport, WA 98548 (206) 877-5254, Staffed information desk, map and book sales, restrooms, pay phone.

Recreation Highlights

Wynoochee Reservoir—This 4.4-mile-long lake is formed by a concrete dam. It provides a pleasant setting for boating, fishing, and swimming. Interpretive exhibits are located at the dam. Camping, picnicking, and hiking opportunities can be found around the lake. South side of the national forest.

Hamma Guard Station—Workers in the Civilian Conservation Corps built this single-story wooden building with gabled roof and hexagonal observation room. The guard station overlooks the Hamma River Valley on the west side of the national forest. Hand-carved shutters and hand-crafted

Children enjoy exploring riparian areas along the many rivers within the national forest. Mike Wewar photo.

iron hinges show the quality workmanship of CCC projects.

Interorrem Guard Station—History buffs may also want to visit this structure built by the Forest Service in 1907. It is one of the oldest national forest buildings still in use in the nation. An interpretive trail and picnic area are located north of the guard station. West side of the national forest.

Campgrounds:

Big Creek—Ten miles northwest of Hoodsport via County Road 44. Twenty-three tent/trailer units, drinking water. Fishing, hunting, hiking, mountain climbing, creek. Elevation 700 feet. Fee.

Brown Creek—Twenty-two miles northwest of Shelton via U.S. 101, forest roads 23 and 2202. Ten tent units and twelve tent/trailer units, drinking water. Fishing, hunting, hiking, swimming, berry picking, stream. Elevation 600 feet. Fee.

Chetwood—Thirty-nine miles north of Montesano via forest roads 22 and 2294. Eight tent units. Hike-in, boat-in, fishing, hiking, swimming, boating, lake. Elevation 800 feet.

Coho—Thirty-eight miles north of Montesano via forest roads 22 and 2294. Twelve picnic sites. Ten tent units and forty-six tent/trailer units, and drinking water. Nature trail, fishing, swimming, boat ramp, group picnic area, lake. Elevation 900 feet. Fee.

Collins—Seven miles west of Brinnon via U.S. Highway 101, County Road 3, and forest road 2510. Two picnic sites. Nine tent units and five tent/trailer units, and drinking water. Elevation 200 feet.

Hamma Hamma—Seven miles northwest of Eldon via U.S. Highway 101 and forest road 25. One picnic site and fifteen tent/trailer units, and drinking water. Fishing, hiking, scenery, mountain climbing, stream. Elevation 600 feet. Fee.

Lena Creek—Eleven miles northwest of Eldon via U.S. Highway 101 and Forest Road 25. Seven tent sites and seven tent/trailer units, and drinking water. Fishing, hunting, hiking, scenery, stream. Elevation 700 feet. Fee.

Resorts and Businesses:

Hoodsport offers groceries, lodging, gas, and laundromat. For more information contact the Mason County Chamber of Commerce at P.O. Box 666, Shelton, WA 98584. (206) 426-2021.

Quilcene Ranger District

The Quilcene Ranger District includes the eastern slopes of Olympic Mountains near Hood Canal.

Information Centers

Quilcene Ranger Station, P.O. Box 280, Quilcene, WA 98376 (206) 765-3368, Staffed information desk, map and book sales, pay phone, restrooms.

Recreation Highlights

Mount Walker Observation Area—Viewpoints at the top of 2,804-foot Mount Walker with views of the Cascade Range including Mount Rainier and Mount Baker. Five million acres of forest; lowlands and Puget Sound visible. Picnic sites, toilets. No water. No camping.

Seal Rock Campground—This site is the only salt-water access in a national forest in Washington State. Visitors harvest oysters along the rocky beach of Hood Canal. The Shell-Midden Interpretive Trail runs 0.25 mile in Douglas-fir forest and along the beach. Signs tell of ancient and modern Indian life and about archaeological findings at the site.

Campgrounds

Dungeness Forks—Eleven miles south of Sequim via U.S. Highway 101

Wildlife species in the national forest include Roosevelt elk and deer like this buck with summer velvet still covering his antlers. Mike Wewar photo.

and Forest Roads 28 and 2880. Nine tent units and drinking water. Fishing, hunting, hiking, stream. Elevation 1,000 feet.

East Crossing—Thirteen miles south of Sequim via U.S. Highway 101, Forest Roads 28 and 2860. Nine tent/trailer units. RVs to sixteen feet. Drinking water. Fishing, hunting, hiking, stream. Elevation 1,200 feet.

Elkhorn—Eleven miles northwest of Brinnon via U.S. Highway 101, County Road 10, and Forest Road 2610. Fourteen tent sites and four tent/trailer units. Fishing, hunting, hiking, scenery, stream. RVs to twenty-one feet. Elevation 600 feet.

Falls View—Four miles southwest of Quilcene via U.S. Highway 101. Four picnic units, five tent units, and thirty tent/trailer units, and drinking water. Hiking, scenery, near Big Quilcene River. Elevation 500 feet. Fee.

Seal Rock—Two miles north of Brinnon via U.S. Highway 101. Ten picnic units, nineteen tent units, and sixteen tent/trailer units, and drinking water. Fishing, beachcombing, boating (no ramp), swimming, Hood Canal. Elevation 100 feet. Fee.

Resorts and Businesses

Towns of **Quilcene**, **Sequim**, and **Port Townsend** offer groceries, gas, lodging, and laundromats. For more information contact the Sequim Chamber of Commerce: P.O. Box 907, Sequim, WA 98382, (206) 683-6197; Port Townsend Chamber of Commerce, 2437 E. Sims Way, Port Townsend, WA 98368, (206) 385-2722.

Soleduck Ranger District

The Soleduck Ranger District includes the western and northern slopes of the Olympic Mountains west of Lake Crescent.

Information Centers

Soleduck Ranger Station, Route 1, Box 5750, Forks, WA 98331 (206) 374-6522, Staffed information desk, map sales, public restrooms.

Recreation Highlights

Lake Crescent—Located within Olympic National Park, an easy drive from Klahowya Campground. This deep glacially-carved lake offers swimming and boating.

Ocean Beaches—There is road access from Forks to the wilderness beaches of Olympic National Park near La Push. Beaches offer swimming, beachcombing, and campground and backcountry camping. Beaches along U.S. Highway 101 offer large Park Service campgrounds with interpretive programs and private resorts, especially near Kalaloch.

Campgrounds

Klahowya—Eight miles east of Sappho via U.S. Highway 101. Thirty-six tent units, thirteen tent/trailer units, drinking water. Fishing, hunting, nature trail, boat ramp. Elevation 800 feet. Fee.

Resorts and Businesses

The towns of **Forks** and **Port Angeles** offer food, gas, lodging, and laundromats. Lake Crescent offers lakeside lodging. For more information contact: Forks Chamber of Commerce, P.O. Box 1249, Forks, WA 98331, (206) 374-2531; Port Angeles Chamber of Commerce, 121 E. Railroad Ave., Port Angeles, WA 98362, (206) 452-2363.

Lake Quinault Ranger District

The Lake Quinault Ranger District includes the western slopes of the

Easy trails for children run along the shores of Lake Quinault and into impressive lowland forests nearby. Mike Wewar photo.

Olympic Mountains near Lake Quinault.

Information Centers

Quinault Ranger Station, Route 1, Box 9, Quinault, WA 98575 (206) 288-2525, Staffed information desk, exhibits, map and book sales, restrooms.

Recreation Highlights

Olympic Rain Forest—The west side of the Olympic Peninsula offers a chance to visit one of the greatest forests on earth. Nature trails wind through lush groves of trees that receive more than 200 inches of rainfall a year.

Lake Quinault—This 200-foot-deep glacially-carved lake is naturally dammed by a glacial moraine. Modern-day glaciers feed the Quinault River and the lake with meltwater. Salmon thrive in the cold water. Scenic drives along the south and north shore of the lake connect to make a loop.

Campgrounds

Campbell Creek Grove—Twenty-five miles northeast of Humptulips via Forest Roads 22 and 2204. Three tent units, eight tent/trailer units, drinking water. Fishing, hunting, hiking. Elevation 1,100 feet.

Falls Creek—0.2 mile northeast of Quinault via the South Shore Quinault Lake Road. Four picnic sites, six tent units, and seventeen tent/trailer units, drinking water. Boat launch, nature trail, swimming, scenery. Elevation 200 feet. Fee.

Gatton Creek—0.3 mile northeast of Quinault via South Shore Lake Quinault Road. Three picnic sites, five tent sites, and seven tent/trailer units, drinking water. Swimming, scenery, lake, creek. RV camping in parking area only. Elevation 200 feet. Fee.

Willaby—0.5 mile southwest of Quinault via South Shore Lake Quinault Road. Five picnic sites, seven tent units, and twelve tent/trailer units. Drinking water and flush toilets. Hiking, swimming, scenery, boat ramp, nature trail, lake. Elevation 200 feet. Fee.

Resorts and Businesses

Lake Quinault Lodge, a historic two-story lodge, is located on the south shore of the lake with hotel rooms and restaurant. **Rain Forest Resort** is a private campground with cabins located on the south shore of the lake. The largest Sitka spruce in the world, sixty feet in girth, is located in the campground.

The town of **Quinault** has a small grocery store and a gas station. The city of **Aberdeen** offers lodging, grocery stores, gas, and laundromats. For more information contact: Grays Harbor Chamber of Commerce, 506 Duffy, Aberdeen, WA 98520, (206) 532-1924.□

Washington Pass Overlook along the North Cascades Scenic Highway offers spectacular views of Liberty Bell Mountain. Forest Service photo.

OKANOGAN NATIONAL FOREST

A stroll through a high meadow in the Okanogan National Forest offers a feast for the senses. A sea of rugged, glaciated peaks in the North Cascades stretches to the west. Gentler foothills, covered with meadows, roll away to the east. The breezes bring scents of wildflowers and fir trees. The sun melts away tension.

The Okanogan National Forest offers miles and miles of trail through mountain meadows, most within the Pasayten Wilderness. Some roads even climb above 6,000 feet, allowing spectacular drives above timberline. The forest has some of the most accessible high country in Washington State. Other trails and roads run through thickets of lodgepole pine, along rocky ridges, and into timbered stream valleys.

There are few glaciers within the Okanogan National Forest, so rivers run clear of glacial sediment and fish thrive. The three major river systems are the Skagit River to the west, the Methow River in the center, and the Okanogan River to the east. The Kettle and Sanpoil rivers drain the extreme eastern part of the national forest.

This national forest lies at some distance from major urban areas, so recreation facilities are generally not overcrowded. There is still a wild, shangri-la quality in places. Small, rustic campgrounds dot riverbanks and lake shores, and a private, peaceful campsite is usually easy to find.

Location

The Okanogan National Forest lies in north-central Washington, sharing its seventy-mile northern border with Canada. The national forest covers the eastern slopes of the North Cascades Mountains south to Lake Chelan and east to the Okanogan River Valley and Okanogan Highlands.

The national forest is bordered on the west by North Cascades National Park, on the east by the Colville National Forest, and on the south by the Wenatchee National Forest.

Towns near the national forest include the larger population centers of Omak and Okanogan and smaller communities of Brewster, Pateros, Twisp, Winthrop, Conconully, Tonasket, and Oroville. Farming, ranching, timber harvest, and recreation support the area's economy.

Visitors reach the national forest via Washington Highway 20, which bisects the forest as it travels west-east from Puget Sound to the Idaho border. The highest portion of Highway 20 is called the North Cascades Scenic Highway. This avalanche-prone section of road is only open from April to November. Many Canadian visitors from the north and visitors from the south travel to the national forest via the north-south highway, U.S. Highway 97.

Climate

Much of the weather in the Okanogan National Forest comes from the Pacific Ocean. Water-saturated clouds blowing in from the west drop most of their moisture as they rise over the Cascade Mountains.

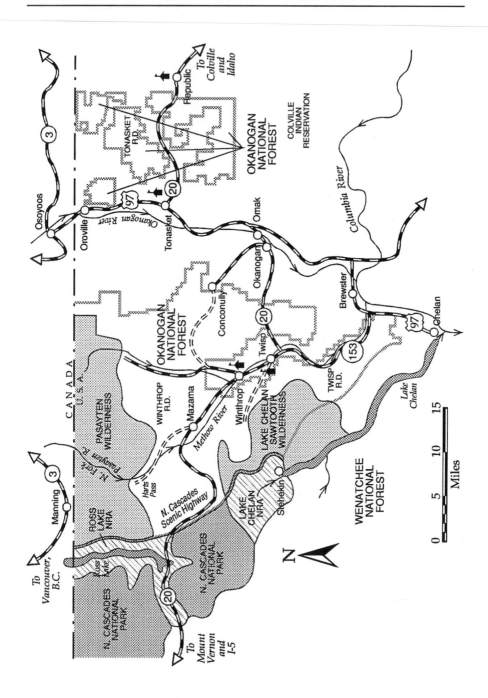

The western portion of the Okanogan National Forest near the Cascade Crest receives much more moisture than the drier eastern portions. Annual precipitation at Rainy Pass in the Cascades averages eighty inches and then declines rapidly eastward to about ten inches near Alta Lake.

Geology

Roadcuts on the North Cascades National Scenic Highway showcase some of the core rocks of the Cascade Mountains. Veins of white quartz criss-cross darker rocks like spider webs. These rocks have been pressure-cooked in the depths of the earth and then shoved upward with the mountains.

The immense spires of granite visible from the highway at Washington Pass are part of the Goldenhorn Batholith, which welled up inside the rising Cascade Range as a huge molten mass of magma and solidified underground. Millions of years of erosion have stripped away softer layers of rock that once covered the batholith, exposing the hard granite to its ice sculptors.

When molten rock rose within the Cascades, hot fluids rich in minerals migrated into cracks in the surrounding rocks. As the fluids cooled, gold, silver, and other minerals crystallized into mineral veins that later lured thousands of prospectors to the North Cascades.

Alpine glaciers carved and continue to carve the craggy peaks of the Cascade Mountains. Huge continental ice sheets ground off sharp mountains to create the more rolling terrain of the Okanogan Highlands. These continental glaciers surged south from Canada several times during the last two-million-year ice age, inundating most of the national forest in an ocean of ice.

Ecology

The national forest shares weather, geology, and ecosystems with Canada. Wildlife and plant species travel back and forth across the international border. Animals rarely found in the continental United States, like lynx, wolves, and grizzly bear, live within the Okanogan National Forest.

Plant and animal associations vary markedly within the national forest depending on rainfall and elevation. The high Cascades receive enough rain to support fir forests; the lower slopes grow ponderosa pine. The drier Okanogan Highlands tend to be covered with fire-prone lodgepole pine forests growing on the tops of hills, with grasslands on the lower slopes.

History

Indians lived in the area now called the Okanogan National Forest for at least 5,000 years. Several tribes used the area seasonally harvesting meat, berries, and fish. Some tribes lived all year in the mountain valleys. They gave the area its first names: Twisp, Methow, Pasayten, Chewack, and Okanogan.

Miners came in the late 1800s, following the fur trappers who told of gold in the Cascades. The place names of their era reflect their purpose: Copper Creek, Gold Ridge, Topaz Mountain. Thousands of mining claims were filed by 1900. But like most Cascades mines, few deposits were concentrated enough to be profitable. By World War I the mining boom had faded and few mines remained in operation. Short tunnels, collapsed shacks, and pieces of rusted machinery are reminders of the era of Cascade gold fever.

The jagged Cascade Mountains surround 7,500-foot Slate Peak near Hart's Pass. The road to Slate Peak offers tremendous views and accesses serveral trailheads for hiking into the Pasayten Wilderness. Curtis Edwards photo.

The peaks of the Lake Chelan-Sawtooth Wilderness rise behind the fertile lowlands of the Methow Valley. The Sawtooth Ridge separates the Methow Valley from Lake Chelan. Curtis Edwards photo.

Modern exploration and extraction techniques brought miners back to the Okanogan National Forest in the 1980s. The national forest has some of the most active mining claims in the state. Modern prospectors have been able to look deeper and longer than their earlier counterparts. Claims in the eastern part of the national forest are rich enough for commercial mining.

Grazing of livestock has been a traditional use of high meadows in the national forest since the turn of the century and was specifically included as an acceptable wilderness use when Congress passed the Wilderness Act in 1964.

Forest-wide Recreation Opportunities

Scenic Drives

North Cascades Scenic Highway—Part of Washington Highway 20 west of Winthrop. Two-lane paved highway over Rainy and Washington passes at the crest of the North Cascades Mountains. Spectacular views and short hikes.

Loup Loup Pass Highway—Part of Washington Highway 20 east of Winthrop. A forty-minute drive through forested mountains on a two-lane paved highway with views of the Cascades and eastern Washington.

Hart's Pass Road—Panoramic views of the Cascade Range from 7,500-foot-high Slate Peak in the North Cascades. Hart's Pass and Slate Peak are reached via Forest Road 5400, a twenty-three mile drive with amazing views and steep drop-offs. The road narrows and turns to gravel for the last fifteen miles. Trailers are not allowed due to safety concerns.

Twisp River Road—Pleasant drive along the Twisp River on Forest Road 4440, mostly gravel. Great views of mountain peaks. Especially scenic in the fall.

Five Lakes Area—Scenic drive east of Tonasket on Highway 20. Turn on County Road 4953 north to Forest Road 32. Bonaparte, Lost, Beaver, Beth, and Little lakes offer fishing, boating, camping, swimming, and hiking. Complete the loop by proceeding through Beaver Canyon and returning through Havillah and Tonasket.

Wilderness areas

Pasayten Wilderness—530,031 acres stretching along the Canadian border in the northern part of the forest. More than 420 miles of maintained trails are open to stock and hikers. Much of the wilderness is meadow country above timberline.

Lake Chelan-Sawtooth Wilderness—95,976 acres of rugged subalpine terrain along the eastern side of Lake Chelan. Many subalpine lakes nestle in meadows around the elevation of 6,000 feet.

Wildlife

Wild lynx cats with tufted ears and very large furry feet live in the Okanogan National Forest. Lynx range south from Canada, stalking their favorite food, the snowshoe hare. The national forest may have the largest concentration of lynx in the continental United States.

Grizzly bear, wolves, and moose live in the northern part of the national forest. Grizzlies and wolves are listed as rare or endangered species and are protected from hunting.

The dry pine forests of eastern Washington provide habitat for rattle-snakes. The Pacific rattlesnake is relatively small and unaggressive and usually will move out of the way with sufficient warning. Walk carefully and avoid snakes, and they will avoid you.

Hunting

One of the largest mule deer populations in the United States is located in the Okanogan National Forest. Deer, upland bird, and bear hunting are popular.

Fishing

Cutthroat and rainbow trout live in most lakes and streams and provide good fishing during legal seasons. Salmon also spawn in many streams in the national forest.

Foraging

Red and blue huckleberries can be found in mid-to late-summer in river valleys and in mountain meadows.

Fall is the best mushroom-picking time for species like shaggy manes and puffballs. Morels are found mostly in late spring and early summer. Mush-rooms are most plentiful in Douglas-fir forests in the valley bottoms.

Permits can be obtained from any ranger station for cutting up to ten cords of wood for home use. Cutting small amounts of dead, downed wood for campfires in campgrounds is allowed.

Water Sports

Rafters, kayakers, and innertube riders enjoy the gentle whitewater of the Methow River during the early summer before water gets too low for navigation.

The lakes of the national forest offer fishing and, in some cases, boating, boat ramps, and swimming. Many of the campgrounds in the national forest are on the shores of small lakes.

Winter Sports

The Methow Valley offers one of the best systems of groomed cross-country ski trails in the nation. The valley offers 150 miles of groomed trails, mostly within the national forest. A non-profit organization maintains the trails and a modest fee is charged for trail use.

A series of European-style backcountry huts in the national forest provides rustic overnight accommodations. Gear is packed from hut to hut in snowmobiles, while guests ski free of heavy backpacks.

Commercial groups offer helicopter skiing adventures for those who wish to be flown to high elevations and then ski down with an experienced guide.

Alpine skiing can be found at Loup Loup Ski Bowl seventeen miles west of Okanogan. This small family-oriented ski area has one poma lift and one rope tow.

Snowmobilers can use 370 miles of groomed trails based out of thirteen Sno-parks.

Off-road Vehicles

All wheeled vehicles including cars, four-wheelers and motorcycles can use forest roads. Motorized vehicles need to be street-legal and drivers must be licensed.

The Twisp Valley has motorbike trails in a few areas, including the Foggy Dew area. Check at the Twisp Ranger Station for more details.

Mountain Bikes

The Methow Valley offers extensive mountain bike routes plus hundreds of miles of forest roads. A guidebook on mountain bike routes is available from Forest Service information centers.The following trips are a just a sampling.

Blackpine Lake—27.5 miles, "more difficult"-rated route on forest roads from Twisp to Blackpine Lake and back. Take County Road 9114, County Road 1071, Forest Road 4300300 to Blackpine Lake. Return on Forest Road 43, County Road 1091, County Road 9114, and County Road 1076.

Buck Lake—Twelve miles on forest roads, including a paved stretch along the Chewuch River and a climb on gravel roads into the Eightmile Creek Valley. Bike up Chewuch Road two miles, left on Road 5130, left on Buck Lake Road 100, left at lake and follow Road 140 until it becomes a jeep track and joins with First Creek Road. Around hillside, down to Cub Creek and to the Chewuch Road.

Bicycling the North Cascades Scenic Highway near Washington Pass allows plenty of time to marvel at the magnificent views of surrounding mountains. Snow lies along the highway well into the summer. Curtis Edwards photo.

Backcountry Travel

The backcountry of the Okanogan National Forest is famous for its long wilderness backpacking trips with many miles of trail in meadows above timberline and through timbered valleys.

More than 1,500 miles of trails are open to foot and horse travel. Most of the trails lie within wilderness areas where motorized and wheeled vehicles are prohibited.

Hikers and riders should carry plenty of water during the summer months as water may be scarce. Be sure to treat water by adding chemicals, boiling, or filtering before drinking.

Non-wilderness Trails

Lake Ann/Maple Pass—Steady uphill walk, 1.9 miles to Lake Ann and 3.1 miles to Maple Pass. Trail keeps an even grade and is appropriate for families. Tremendous views and good fishing. Open to hikers only. No camping within 0.25 mile of Lake Ann. Trailhead off Highway 20 at Rainy Pass.

Lookout Mountain—Moderately steep trail, 1.3 miles to a fire lookout tower on top of Lookout Mountain. One hour hike, view of Sawtooth Ridge and valleys. Open to horses, bicycles, and motorbikes. There is no water. Trailhead up Forest Road 44 to Forest Road 4345200.

Wilderness Trails:

The Lake Chelan-Sawtooth Wilderness and Pasayten Wilderness have a party-size limitation of twelve people and eighteen head of stock.

Horseshoe Basin Trail—Trailhead is twenty miles northeast of Tonasket. This gentle, five-mile trail is one of the easiest ways for riders and hikers to reach the miles and miles of rolling meadows of the eastern Pasayten Wilderness. Sheep sometimes are grazed, under permit, in Horseshoe Basin.

War Creek Trail—Off the Twisp River Road. This trail serves as a portal to the Lake Chelan-Sawtooth Wilderness. After nine miles of moderate climbing, the trail reaches War Creek Pass and dips down into the Lake Juanita Basin, a meadowed dimple at the ridgetop. The trail then climbs back up to Purple Pass for view down to fifty-five-mile-long Lake Chelan and the mountains beyond.

Horse Trails—The wilderness areas of the Okanogan National Forest provide many miles of horse trails. Some trailheads have horse camps nearby, stock-loading platforms, and hitching rails.

Check district information centers for detailed information about which trails are open to horses.

Mountain Climbing

Most technical mountain climbing opportunities are focused in the North Cascades portion of the national forest near the crest of the mountains. Peaks such as Liberty Bell and Silver Star near Washington Pass require rock and snow climbing gear, training, and experience. Excellent climbing guides are published for the North Cascades. Climbers should consult a guide before attempting peaks in the national forest.

Barrier-free Sites

All visitor information centers and most restrooms and campgrounds have barrier-free access.

Rainy Lake Trail—This flat, one-mile, paved trail leads from 4,000-foot Rainy Pass to Rainy Lake. Trail offers great views of massive peaks rising behind the lake and a waterfall plunging from the cliffs into the lake. Trail has frequent benches and interpretive signs.

Washington Pass Overlook—0.25-mile paved trail to spectacular views of Liberty Bell Mountain.

Children's Activities

Hiking the **Rainy Lake Trail** can be an enjoyable family activity due to the level, safe trail and interesting interpretive signs. The trail is located just off the North Cascades Scenic Highway and makes a good travel break for car-weary children.

Slate Peak Lookout, near Hart's Pass, is a safe but steep road walk to a fire tower with 360-degree views of the North Cascades Mountains. Children enjoy finding marine fossils in the slate rocks along the walk to the lookout

Rainy Lake Trail offers unique hiking opportunities. Nearly a mile of the trail is paved and accessible for the physically challenged. Forest Service photo.

and reading the interpretive signs at the summit.

Pearrygin Lake is a Washington State Park just outside the forest boundary near Winthrop. The lake has an excellent swimming beach with reasonably warm water and acres of lawns for kids to play tag or catch. Pay showers are available in the dressing rooms. Other state parks with similar features in Okanogan County include Alta Lake near Pateros, Osoyoos, north of Oroville, and Conconully, seventeen miles northwest of Okanogan.

Forest Headquarters

Okanogan National Forest Headquarters, 1240 Second Ave. S, Okanogan, Wash., 98840, (509) 826-3275.

Ranger District Recreation Opportunities

Winthrop Ranger District

The Winthrop District includes the Methow and Chewuch River watersheds on the east slopes of the Cascade Mountains and the upper part of the Skagit River drainage just west of the Cascade crest. Terrain varies from glaciated mountains to dry pine-covered hillsides. Snow lies late in the high country.

Information Centers

Winthrop Ranger Station, W. Chewuch Rd., Winthrop, Wash., 98862, (509) 996-2266. Staffed information desk, map and book sales, restroom, and free literature.

Early Winters Visitor Information Center, Highway 20, Mazama, Wash. Staffed information desk, map and book sales, restroom, and free literature. Open daily Memorial Day weekend through Labor Day.

Washington Pass Visitor Information Center Highway 20. Staffed information booth, map and book sales, restroom, and free literature. Open daily Memorial Day weekend through Labor Day.

Recreation Highlights

Washington Pass Scenic Overlook—Along the North Cascades Scenic Highway. This viewpoint offers spectacular views of Liberty Bell Mountain and Early Winters Spires. Interpretive services, picnic area, visitor information booth, and a short, barrier-free trail. Highway open April-November.

Hart's Pass—Panoramic views of the Cascade Range from this 7,500-foot-high mountain-meadow trailhead for the Pacific Crest Trail. Trailhead reached via a twenty-three mile drive on a paved and gravel road with amazing views and steep drop-offs.

North Cascades Smokejumper Base—Four miles south of Winthrop on County Road 9129. The base is the birthplace of the Forest Service smokejumper program. Visitors welcome to tour the base in the summer.

Campgrounds

Ballard—Twenty-two miles northwest of Winthrop via State Highway 20, County Road 1163, and Forest Road 5400. Six units. Fishing. Elevation 2,600 feet.

Buck Lake—Twelve miles north of Winthrop via County Road 9137 and Forest Roads 51, 5130, 100, and 5130100. Nine tent units. RVs to sixteen feet. Boating, fishing. Elevation 3,200 feet.

Camp 4—Eighteen miles northeast of Winthrop via County Road 9137 and Forest Road 51. Five tent units. Fishing. Elevation 2,400 feet.

Chewuch—Fifteen miles north of Winthrop via County Road 9137 and Forest Road 51. Four tent units, two on the river. Campground sees little use. RVs to sixteen feet. Fishing. Elevation 2,200 feet.

Early Winters—Seven tent units and six tent/trailer units, drinking water, RVs to sixteen feet. Fishing. Fee. Elevation 2,400 feet.

Falls Creek—Eleven miles north of Winthrop via County Road 9137 and Forest Road 51. Four tent units and three tent/trailer units along Chewuch

Forest roads weave through the mountains of the Okanogan National Forest, providing miles and miles of restful scenic drives. Curtis Edwards photo.

River, RVs to sixteen feet. Fishing, 0.25-mile hike to waterfall. Elevation 2,300 feet.

Flat—Eleven miles north of Winthrop via County Road 9137 and Forest Roads 51 and 5130. Nine tent units and three tent/trailer units, RVs to sixteen feet. Fishing. Elevation 2,600 feet.

Hart's Pass—Thirty-three miles northwest of Winthrop via State Highway 20, County Road 1163, and Forest Road 5400. The road is narrow, partly gravel, and closed to trailers. Five tent units. Alpine meadows, access to Pacific Crest Trail. Elevation 6,200 feet.

Honeymoon—Eighteen miles northwest of Winthrop via County Road 9137 and Forest Roads 51 and 5130. Six tent/trailer units. Fishing. Elevation 3,300 feet.

Klipchuck—Nineteen miles northwest of Winthrop on State Highway 20. Six tent units and forty tent/trailer units, drinking water. Fishing and hiking. Units can be combined to accommodate groups. Fee. Elevation 3,000 feet.

Lone Fir—Twenty-seven miles northwest of Winthrop on State Highway 20. Twenty-one tent sites and six tent/trailer sites, drinking water. Fishing and hiking. Fee. Elevation 3,800 feet.

Meadows—Thirty-four miles northwest of Winthrop via County Road 1163 and Forest Roads 5400 and 5400500. Access road is closed to trailers. Fourteen tent units. Alpine meadows, access to Pacific Crest Trail. Elevation 6,200 feet.

Nice—Thirteen miles north of Winthrop via County Road 9137 and forest roads 51 and 5130. Four tent units. Fishing. Elevation 2,700 feet.

River Bend—Twenty-three miles northwest of Winthrop via County Road 1163 and Forest Road 5400. Five tent units. Fishing and hiking. Elevation 2,700 feet.

Ruffed Grouse—Seventeen miles northwest of Winthrop via County Road 9137 and forest roads 51 and 5130. Four tent units. Fishing. Elevation 3,200 feet.

Dispersed Sites—Riverfront camp areas can be found along the Methow and Chewuch Rivers.

Other Campgrounds

Pearrygin State Park—Located two miles northeast of Winthrop near the national forest boundary. Higher-priced than Forest Service campgrounds, but includes hook-ups, showers, drinking water, swimming beach, and lawn-covered lake shore.

Alta Lake State Park—Located near Pateros at the southern end of the national forest. Similar amenities to Pearrygin State Park.

Resorts and Businesses

Winthrop: town has an old-west theme and caters to almost every tourist need. Winthrop can provide lodging, food, groceries, and gas. There are souvenir stores, a bookstore, a museum, and a library. A grocery and hardware store two miles east of town provide lower-cost necessities.

Sun Mountain Lodge–an upscale European-style lodge located on a hillside to the south of Winthrop. Views of the mountains from the lodge. Overnight accommodations, restaurant, winter cross-country ski packages, groomed trails, ski rentals.

Outfitters and guides are available for cross-country skiing, and rafting trips into the national forest. Contact Forest Service offices for details.

Twisp Ranger District

The Twisp District includes the Twisp River watershed and the Sawtooth Mountains on the southeast side of Lake Chelan. Terrain varies from mountain crags and dry, rugged ridgetops to pine-covered hillsides and forested river valleys.

Information Centers

Twisp Ranger Station, 502 Glover, Twisp, WA, 98856, (509) 997-2131. Staffed information desk, map and book sales, restrooms, and free literature.

Recreation Highlights

Gilbert Mining Camp—Turn-of-the-century mining camp that once had a population of 1,500, located along the Twisp River. Two cabins and the remains of others can be seen.

Twisp River—Major attraction for water sports, especially fishing.

Buttermilk Butte—High-elevation point at the end of a road providing views of Methow Valley and Sawtooth Ridge.

Lookout Mountain Lookout—Operating fire lookout during the summer. Accessed by 1.3 miles of trail.

Campgrounds

Black Pine Lake—Nineteen miles southwest of Twisp via County Road 9114 and Forest Road 43. One picnic site, three tent units and twenty-three tent/trailer units. Drinking water. Boating, fishing, and hiking. No gas engines on boats on lake. Fee. Elevation 4,200 feet.

Foggy Dew—Nine miles southwest of Carlton via county roads 1029 and 1034 and Forest Road 4340. Thirteen tent/trailer units. Motorbike trails. Elevation 2,400 feet.

JR—Twelve miles east of Twisp on State Highway 20. Six tent/trailer units, drinking water. Fee. Elevation 3,900 feet.

Loup Loup—Thirteen miles east of Twisp via State Highway 20 and Forest Road 42. Four tent units and twenty tent/trailer units. Group picnic area. Drinking water. Fee. Elevation 4,200 feet.

Mystery—Eighteen miles west of Twisp via County Road 9114 and Forest Road 44. Four tent/trailer units. Fishing and hiking. Elevation 2,800 feet.

Poplar Flat—Twenty miles west of Twisp via County Road 9114 and forest roads 44 and 4440. Three picnic sites and fifteen tent/trailer units. Drinking water, picnic area, and community kitchen. Fishing, hiking. Fee. Elevation 2,900 feet.

Roads End—Twenty-five miles west of Twisp via County Road 9114 and forest roads 44 and 4440. Four tent/trailer units, RVs under sixteen feet. Fishing and hiking. Elevation 3,600 feet.

South Creek—Twenty-two miles west of Twisp via County Road 9114 and forest roads 44 and 4440. Four tent/trailer units, RVs under sixteen feet. Fishing and hiking. Fee. Elevation 3,100 feet.

Twisp River Horse Camp—Twenty-two miles west of Twisp via county roads 9114 and 1090 and forest roads 4430 and 4435. Twelve tent/trailer units. Elevation 3,100 feet.

War Creek—Fourteen miles west of Twisp via County Road 9114 and Forest Road 44. Eleven tent/trailer units, drinking water. Fishing and hiking. Fee. Elevation 2,400 feet.

Resorts and Businesses

Twisp offers food, groceries, gas, lodging, and laundromat.

Loup Loup Ski Area is a downhill ski area commercially run within the national forest. Access from Highway 20, thirty minutes east of Twisp. Small family ski area. Low prices for lift tickets.

Tonasket Ranger District

The Tonasket District includes the tree-crowned, grassy-sided hills of the Okanogan Highlands, which lie primarily east of the Okanogan River.

Families enjoy picnics and fishing at Lost Lake within the Tonasket Ranger District. Forest Service photo.

Information Centers
Tonasket Ranger Station, 1 W. Winesap, Tonasket, Wash., 98855, (509) 486-2186. Staffed information desk, map sales, restrooms.

Recreation Highlights
Big Tree Botanical Area—One mile northeast of Lost Lake. An easy fifteen-minute hike to large specimens of native western larch trees.

Lost Lake, Bonaparte Lake, and other district lakes—Focus for water sports within the district. Very popular during hot summer months.

Pasayten Wilderness—Eastern access points for many wilderness trails. Weather tends to be better on the east side of the wilderness. Attracts early-season hikers due to early snow-melt.

Okanogan Historical Museum—Displays of historical items from the local area and photographs. Located in Okanogan on Business Alternate Highway 97.

Molson Museum and Old Molson—Historic site of former boomtown of Molson. Located in the Okanogan Highlands fifteen miles east of Oroville.

Campgrounds
Beaver Lake—Thirty-four miles northeast of Tonasket via State Highway 20, County Road 4953, and Forest Road 32. One picnic unit, three tent units, one tent/trailer unit, drinking water. Boating, fishing, swimming, and hiking. Fee. Elevation 3,000 feet.

Beth Lake—Thirty-four miles northeast of Tonasket via State Highway 20, County Road 4953, Forest Road 32, and County Road 9480. Three picnic sites and seventeen tent/trailer units. Drinking water. Boating, fishing, swimming, and hiking. Fee. Elevation 2,900 feet.

Bonaparte Lake—Twenty-six miles northeast of Tonasket via State Highway 20, County Road 4953, and Forest Road 32. Seven picnic sites and twenty-five tent/trailer units. Drinking water and group picnic area. Boating, fishing, swimming, hiking. Fee. Elevation 3,600 feet.

Cottonwood—Two miles north of Conconully via Forest Road 38. One tent unit and four tent/trailer units, drinking water. Fishing. Fee. Elevation 2,700 feet.

Crawfish Lake—Twenty miles east of Riverside via County Road 9320 and forest roads 30 and 30100. Five picnic sites and twenty-two tent/trailer units. Boating, fishing, and waterskiing. Elevation 4,500 feet.

Kerr—Four miles northwest of Conconully via Forest Road 38. Nine tent/trailer units. Fishing. Elevation 3,100 feet.

Lost Lake—Nineteen miles north of Wauconda via State Highway 20, County Road 4953, and forest roads 32, 33, and 32050. Thirteen picnic sites and twenty tent/trailer units. Drinking water and group picnic area. Boating, fishing, swimming, and hiking. Fee. Elevation 3,800 feet.

Lyman Lake—Twenty-eight miles southeast of Tonasket via State Highway 20, county roads 9455 and 3785. Six tent/trailer units. Fishing and swimming. Elevation 2,900 feet.

Oriole—Three miles northwest of Conconully via Forest Roads 38 and 38025. Two tent units, six tent/trailer units and drinking water. Fishing. Fee. Elevation 2,900 feet.

The Chewuch River near Camp 4. Small campgrounds are available along the river.
Curtis Edwards photo.

Salmon Meadows—Nine miles northwest of Conconully via Forest Road 38. One picnic site and fourteen tent units. Drinking water and community kitchen. Hiking. Fee. Elevation 4,500 feet.

Sugarloaf—Five miles northeast of Conconully via County Road 4015. Four tent units, one tent/trailer unit, and drinking water. Boating, swimming, and fishing. Elevation 2,400 feet.

Sweat Creek—Thirty-one miles east of Tonasket on State Highway 20. Five picnic units and nine tent/trailer units. Drinking water. Fee. Elevation 3,500 feet.

Tiffany Springs—Thirty-one miles northwest of Conconully via County Road 2017 and Forest Roads 37 and 39. Six tent/trailer units, RVs to sixteen feet. Hiking. Elevation 6,800 feet.

Other Campgrounds:

RV park located in Omak on the east side of Okanogan River. Offers showers, water, electricity, and sewage hook-ups. Near Omak Stampede Grounds. Fee.

Okanogan Legion Park has trailer parking, showers, and restrooms. Located in north Okanogan along the Okanogan River. Fee.

Tonasket Information Center has a camping and RV area. No hookups.

Resorts and Businesses

Okanogan, **Omak**, and **Tonasket** offer food, groceries, gas, lodging, and laundromat.☐

NOTES

Mt. Baker, smothered in glaciers, rises to 10,778 feet above sea level in the northern part of the Mount Baker-Snoqualmie National Forest. Jim Hughes, Forest Service photo.

MOUNT BAKER-SNOQUALMIE NATIONAL FOREST

The Mount Baker-Snoqualmie National Forest includes breath-taking natural wonders of the North Cascades Mountains: immense glacier-covered volcanos, mountain meadows ablaze with wildflowers, and dark forests, thick with huge old trees:

The North Cascades are the highest and most rugged mountains in the Cascade Range. Ice-age glaciers carved the rocky crags, and hundreds of active glaciers and countless streams, rivers, and waterfalls continue the geologic sculpting processes today. Valley bottoms lie near sea level, while mountain tops rise to over 10,000 feet.

People come from all over the world to visit these "American Alps." The mountains in the Mount Baker-Snoqualmie National Forest offer rock and ice climbing, wilderness hiking, whitewater rafting, fishing, hunting, and all kinds of skiing. Scenic drives take visitors to spectacular vistas, and peaceful, forested campgrounds allow respite after busy days.

Location

The 1.7 million acres of the Mount Baker-Snoqualmie National Forest cover the western slopes of the Cascade Mountains for 130 miles, from the Canadian border south to Mount Rainier National Park. The national forest is a short drive from Seattle and many other large cities of the Puget Sound area.

Six major rivers in the national forest flow west from the crest of the Cascades to the Puget Sound lowlands. Each river flows in a steep-sided glacial valley. These valleys create self-contained recreation packages with campgrounds, trails, picnic areas, and information stations. Most of the valleys dead-end in steep, mountainous terrain.

The Mount Baker-Snoqualmie National Forest borders North Cascades National Park in the northern section of the forest and Mount Rainier National Park in the south. Regulations and land management policies vary between the parks and the national forest.

Climate

Climate varies markedly within the Mount Baker-Snoqualmie National Forest from the glaciated mountaintops to the tree-covered valley bottoms. The Cascades create their own weather by snagging Pacific Ocean storms. Huge masses of clouds saturated with water roll in off the Pacific and slam into the mountain range most of the year. The clouds rise, cool, and drop their moisture as rain or snow. Valley bottoms, near the western edge of the forest, receive only thirty to sixty inches of rain a year while higher elevations may receive over 500 inches, mostly in the form of snow. Twenty feet of snow on the ground is common during most winters at higher elevations. In some areas, snow doesn't melt until mid-summer.

MOUNT BAKER-SNOQUALMIE
NATIONAL FOREST

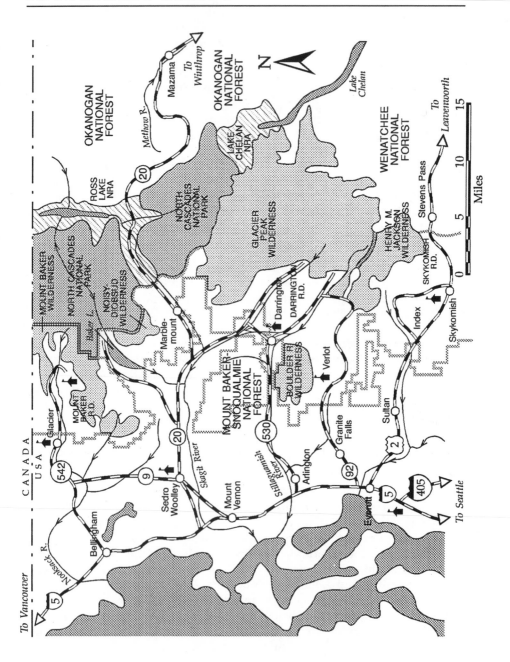

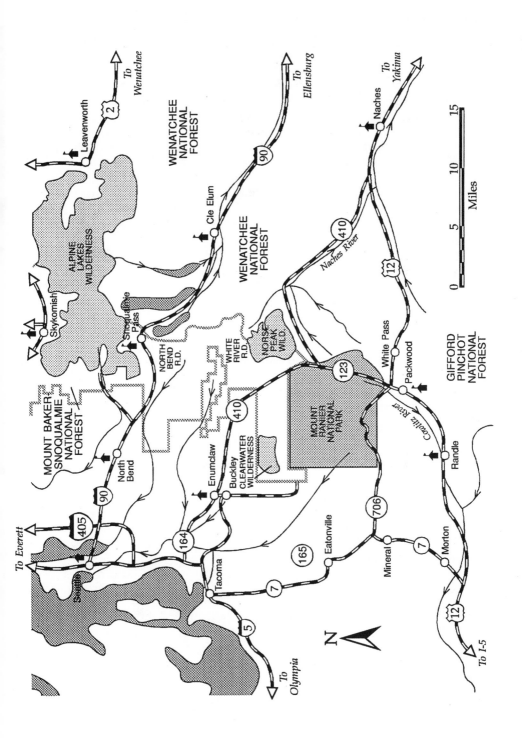

Geology

Two volcanos rise above the rest of the mountains within the national forest. Mount Baker, at 10,778 feet, provides the headwaters for the Nooksack River near the Canadian Border. Glacier Peak, at 10,568 feet, lies fifty miles south, deep within the Glacier Peak Wilderness. These volcanos have erupted many times during the past few hundred thousand years, filling mountain valleys with lava flows and sending huge clouds of ash skyward.

Glacier Peak has been dormant for thousands of years and glaciers have deeply eroded its flanks. Mount Baker last erupted around 100 years ago and steam still pours from the active vent in its crater. Geologists monitor Mount Baker, watching for any further signs that this volcano might be waking up like its cousin to the south, Mount St. Helens.

The rest of the mountains in the national forest are made of much older rocks than the relatively young volcanic peaks. The North Cascades are a complex jumble of metamorphic, sedimentary and volcanic rocks that have been folded and faulted during six million years of mountain building. The oldest rocks date from the precambrian era, more than 600 million years ago.

Some geologists think that many of the rocks in the North Cascade mountain range were once islands in the south Pacific that floated northeastward on the conveyer belt of the moving Pacific Ocean floor. When the islands reached North America, they collided with the continent and were attached to the mainland.

Ice-age continental glaciers surged south from Canada several times in the last two million years. These huge ice sheets filled the river valleys and flowed up and over some ridges grinding off their rough edges, especially in the northern portion of the national forest. Glaciers filled the valley of the North Fork of the Nooksack River to around 7,000 feet. Today, ridges below 7,000 feet tend to be rounded, while higher ridges retain their edges, peaks, and angular lines.

The ice-age ice sheets melted away around 10,000 years ago, leaving behind a legacy of U-shaped valleys, rounded ridges, lake basins, and gravel moraines. Smaller alpine glaciers continue to carve away at the highest peaks today, mostly on north-facing slopes near the summits. These modern-day glaciers function as water reservoirs. They accumulate snow and ice during the winter and then melt during the summer, slowly releasing water to keep the rivers full even during the dry months of July and August.

Ecology

In the national forest, ecosystems vary with elevation. The rivers and streams that thunder down the valleys provide aquatic habitat for trout and salmon. Bald eagle and osprey feed on the fish.

The thick volcanic soils of the lower slopes and valley bottoms grow Douglas fir and western hemlock. The trees provide shelter for birds such as varied thrush and spotted owls and animals like black bear and black-tailed deer. Other animals such as mountain goats use these forests for winter habitat.

Silver fir and mountain hemlock trees adapt to the longer winters of higher elevations by growing in shapes that shed snow and elude wind. At timberline, trees grow smaller and cluster on humps and ridges that melt free of snow early each spring. Timberline trees grow slowly, sometimes living more than 1,000 years.

Above timberline and below the glaciers, meadow plants grow among the rocks and small mountain lakes. Plants like heather and huckleberry avoid wind and cold by growing close to the ground. A blanket of snow protects them during the winter. Animals such as marmot and mountain goat feed in the meadows during the two-month summers but hibernate or migrate to lower elevations after the snow falls.

The glacial ice and wind-scoured rock of the highest elevations provide few niches for life. Only organisms like ice worms and lichens can adapt to the year-round wintery temperatures and howling winds.

History

The Mount Baker-Snoqualmie National Forest has been the ancestral hunting, gathering, and ceremonial grounds for several Indian tribes for more than 5,000 years. Indians harvested berries, roots, deer, bear, mountain goat, cedar, and salmon. Many of the place names in the national forest, such as Stillaguamish and Shuksan, are derived from the original Indian names. Tribes still use the forests today and retain treaty rights to some special uses.

Early non-Indian explorers arrived in the 1800s, including trappers, miners, and army engineers searching for railroad routes over the Cascade Mountains. A brief mining boom in the late 1800s opened up many of the trails and roads in use today, although most miners came away with only

The Civilian Conservation Corps built the Glacier Public Service Center during the Great Depression. The Cascadian-style architecture was typical of CCC projects in the Pacific Northwest. Jim Hughes, Forest Service photo.

broken dreams. In the late 1800s, railroads like the Great Northern Railway overcame the towering natural obstacles of the mountains with miles of snowsheds, tunnels, and huge wooden trestles.

During the early part of the twentieth century, people began to discover the recreation opportunities of the national forest. Luxury mountain lodges like the Mount Baker Lodge and Big Four Inn hosted tourists from all over the country until they burned down or were put out of business by a world war or the depression.

Climbing groups like the Mountaineers or the Mazamas, out of Oregon, came to the forest to climb peaks, often with 100 people in a climbing party. Skiing became popular in the 1940s and 1950s, and many commercial ski areas were developed within the national forests. Most of these ski areas have expanded and modernized and still operate today.

The Civilian Conservation Corps, a government work program during the Great Depression, built many of the historical structures still standing within the national forest. Some of these structures have been restored so visitors can appreciate the beauty and utility of their Cascadian architecture and the craftsmanship of the builders.

Forest-wide Recreation Opportunities

Scenic Drives

The **Mount Baker Scenic Byway**, twenty-four miles at the western end of State Highway 542 on the slopes of Mount Baker, is a paved, two-lane road with dizzying switchbacks. Highlights include spectacular views of the crags and glaciers of 9,127-foot Mount Shuksan and other Nooksack Valley peaks including Mount Baker. Side trips on single-lane logging roads lead to 175-foot-high Nooksack Falls and to the incredible close-up views of Mount Baker offered by the Mount Baker Vista.

The **Mountain Loop Scenic Byway**, in the Darrington Ranger District, is a fifty-mile winding drive from Granite Falls to Darrington. The route leads through dense forests and past rivers with whitewater rapids and deep green pools. It offers views of craggy peaks and hanging waterfalls. Three self-guided interpretive trails offer exhibits explaining the natural and human history of the area. Portions of the road are gravel.

The **Stevens Pass Scenic Byway**, in the Skykomish Ranger District, is a sixty-nine-mile section of Highway 2, the main east-west highway between Everett and Wenatchee. The byway runs along whitewater rivers, beneath sheer mountain cliffs, and through the Stevens Pass Historic District where roadside signs and trails interpret railroad history.

The **Mather Memorial Parkway**, in the White River Ranger District, is a fifty-three mile stretch of Highway 410 east of Enumclaw, designated a parkway in 1931 to preserve its scenic beauty. The route offers views of elk grazing, the free-flowing upper sections of White River, old-growth forests, and the immense snowy summit of Mount Rainier.

Wild and Scenic Rivers

Skagit Wild and Scenic River—158 miles of the Skagit River set aside for its outstanding scenic, natural, and cultural values. This free-flowing system includes portions of the Skagit, Cascade, Suiattle, and Sauk rivers. Activities include bald eagle watching, fishing, and rafting. Other rivers within the national forest have been proposed for wild and scenic status.

Wilderness Areas

Nearly forty-two percent of the national forest is Congressionally-designated wilderness. Five hundred eighty miles of trails provide access to the eight wilderness areas. Wilderness hikers should be prepared for stream-fording, route-finding, and primitive campsites. Outfitter-guides provide commercial pack trips and hikes.

Mount Baker Wilderness 122,676 acres
Noisy-Diobsud Wilderness 15,015 acres
Boulder River Wilderness 50,388 acres
Glacier Peak Wilderness 282,267 acres
Henry M. Jackson Wilderness 75,836 acres
Alpine Lakes Wilderness 145,358 acres
Clearwater Wilderness 14,255 acres
Norse Peak Wilderness 15,923 acres.

Wildlife

Hundreds of bald eagles feed on salmon in the Nooksack and Skagit rivers during the fall and winter. Eagle-watching sites along the Skagit River offer interpretive exhibits. Commercial eagle-watching raft trips are available. Other birds within the national forest include golden eagle, varied thrush, water ouzel, northern spotted owl, great horned owl, red-tailed hawk, great blue heron, grouse, ptarmigan, raven, hummingbird, and several species of swallow.

Elk and deer can be seen browsing in lowland open areas. Marmots, pika, and mountain goat can be viewed in most subalpine areas, especially the Heather Meadows day-use area. Wolves are returning to the northern portions of the national forest and are protected from hunting. Other mammals in the national forest include ground squirrel, vole, rabbit, bobcat and cougar.

Spawning salmon fill the tributary streams of the rivers during the late summer and fall. Salmon fishing is prohibited in spawning areas. Other fish in the national forest include bulltrout, cutthroat trout, rainbow trout, and steelhead.

Amphibians in the national forest include tailed frogs, a primitive frog that lives in very cold streams and takes up to seven years to reach maturity. Other reptiles and amphibians include giant salamander, long-toed salamander, tree frog, and garter snake. There are no poisonous snakes in the national forest. Some species like the Cascades frog are found only in the southern parts of the national forest due to species eradication during the heavy ice-age glaciation of the more northern areas.

Hunting

Deer, elk, black bear, and grouse are the most common game species within the national forest. Hunting licenses are required and Washington State hunting regulations apply. Hunting seasons for most species are in the fall.

Fishing

Anglers are most likely to catch rainbow or cutthroat trout in the lakes and streams of the national forest. Streams fed by glaciers tend to be clouded by glacial silt and do not provide good fishing. Streams fed by snowmelt have much clearer water and sustain larger fish populations.

Foraging

Berries at the lower elevations ripen in July and include high-bush huckleberries, wild blackberries, thimbleberries, and black caps. Good berry picking areas include the Baker Lake area in the Mount Baker District, Green Mountain in the Darrington District, Tonga Ridge in the Skykomish District, Stampede Pass in the North Bend District, and Suntop in the White River District. Higher-elevation low-bush huckleberries ripen in August. Good subalpine picking areas include Heather Meadows and other mountain meadows.

Most mushrooms pop up after the autumn rains in the lowland forest areas. Favorite picking varieties include chanterelles, boletes, and coral mushrooms. Some species are deadly. Only pick mushrooms you are sure are edible.

Water Recreation

Whitewater rafting and kayaking are challenging in spring and early summer when melting snow turns the rivers into boiling cauldrons of rapids and whirlpools. Some rivers flow over high waterfalls. Only experienced whitewater boaters should attempt the rivers of the national forest. Guided raft trips are available from trained outfitter/guides. By late summer many rivers are too low for rafting.

The swimming beach at Horseshoe Cove Campground at Baker Lake is the only formal swimming area in the national forest. It has a sandy beach and buoys to define shallow water but no lifeguards. Swimming is allowed in other lakes, but the water is very cold all year.

Winter Recreation

Seven alpine ski areas within the national forest provide downhill skiing each winter. Most areas open after Thanksgiving and close in April. Snow is usually plentiful but wet. Prepare for falling snow or rain.

The **Mount Baker Ski Area** is located at the east end of State Highway 542. It is open for day skiing only. The area offers spectacular views of Mount Baker and Mount Shuksan.

The **Stevens Pass Ski Area** is located on State Highway 2 east of Everett at Stevens Pass. It offers day and night skiing, seven days a week, twenty-six major runs and great views of surrounding mountains.

The **Snoqualmie Summit Ski Area, Alpental Ski Area, Hyak Ski Area, and Ski Acres Ski Area** are all located on Interstate 90 east of Seattle. They offer day and night skiing, seven days a week within 1.5 hours of Seattle. Many ski schools operate in the ski areas.

The **Crystal Mountain Ski Area** is located on State Highway 410 east of Enumclaw. The area offers overnight lodging and day and night skiing seven days a week and ten chair lifts. Skiers enjoy panoramic views of Mount

Rainier from the upper portions of ski runs.

Snow-covered forest roads offer cross-country skiing, snowshoeing, and snowmobiling from October through April. Some areas are closed to snow-mobiles. Avalanche danger is extreme at some times during the snow season. Check at Forest Service offices for current conditions.

Groomed cross-country ski trails are available for a small fee at the margins of most downhill ski areas including Ski Acres, Stevens Pass, Crystal Mountain, and Mount Baker. The trails and open meadow areas of the Mount Baker National Recreation Area are open to snowmobiles.

Off-road Vehicles

Twenty-five miles of trail are designated for off-road vehicles within the national forest. ORVs also use the hundreds of miles of minimally maintained gravel forest roads. If the vehicle is not licensed for highway use it must have a Washington State ORV permit tab and be street legal. Drivers must be state licensed. The Evans Creek Campground in the White River District offers adjacent ORV trails.

Backcountry Travel

Trails in the national forest tend to climb from roadside trailheads up to meadows, ridges, and peaks. Most trails outside wilderness areas are relatively short, with three-to five-mile hikes common. Trails within wilderness areas tend to begin with long up and down walks along rivers or streams and then climb to higher elevation destinations like lakes or peaks. There are almost 1,500 miles of trail within the national forest.

Other guides and maps provide extensive information about hiking in the national forest. The following suggestions are just a sampler of available opportunities.

Non-wilderness Trails

Noisy-Diobsud—Trail begins at the end of the Anderson Creek Road, Forest Road 1107, on the east side of Baker Lake. Route climbs gently through timber and meadows to two groups of alpine lakes. 2.5 miles. Mount Baker District.

East Bank—Trail begins a mile up Forest Road 1107 on the east side of Baker Lake. An easy hike along the shore of Baker Lake passing through an old forest fire scar caused by the 1843 eruption of Mount Baker. Four miles. Mount Baker District.

Wagon Road Trail—Trail begins near the Denny Creek Campground three miles off I-90 via exit 47 and Forest Road 58. A short, easy hike along the original Snoqualmie Pass Wagon Road. Two mile loop through mostly old-growth forest. North Bend District.

Goat Falls Trail—Trail begins a mile off State Highway 410 via forest roads 7174 and 7174410. Route travels through part of the Silver Springs Summer Home area, crosses Goat Creek on a foot bridge and then continues for a half mile through old-growth to a small waterfall. White River District.

Wilderness Trails

Chain Lakes—This popular loop trail begins and ends at Heather Meadows and passes through part of the Mount Baker Wilderness. Two miles of

Boardwalks allow wheelchair access to trails like this barrier-free route around Picture Lake at Heather Meadows. Jim Hughes, Forest Service photo.

road separate the two trailheads. The trail traverses rock cliffs and winds past a series of alpine lakes. Seven miles. Mount Baker District.

Slide Lake—Beginning near the end of Forest Road 16, the trail enters the Glacier Peak Wilderness and tree-lined Slide Lake. Numerous wilderness high lakes can be reached by bushwhacking cross-country from Slide Lake. One mile to Slide Lake. Mount Baker District.

Goat Lake/Elliot Creek—Trail begins four miles off the Mountain Loop Highway via Forest Road 4080. The five-mile route follows Elliot Creek through and old-growth forest, an old clearcut, and then follows an old puncheon wagon road to sixty-four-acre Goat Lake, a lovely mountain lake at the base of towering mountains. Darrington District.

Clearwater—Trail begins fifteen miles off Highway 410 via Forest Road 74 and a short distance up the Carbon Trail 1179. Eight somewhat difficult miles through old-growth forest and mountain meadows. White River District. All wilderness areas have a twelve-person party-size limitation.

Mountain Climbing

The two highest peaks in the national forest, Mount Baker (10,778 feet) and Glacier Peak (10,550 feet) each have multiple climbing routes. The standard route on each mountain is relatively easy, requiring only a rope, ice axe, and crampons. Climbers attempting those peaks should have some climbing experience. Other routes vary from easy to extremely difficult. Most climbers attempt the peaks in the spring and summer when weather is more likely to be good. In late summer, the snow bridges over crevasses melt away and route-finding becomes challenging.

Other climbing challenges include Mount Shuksan (9,127 feet), Whitehorse Mountain (6,852 feet), and Sloan Peak (7,835 feet). Rock climbing skills and equipment are necessary for these peaks.

Barrier-free Sites

All visitor information centers provide barrier-free access to exhibits, sales areas, information desk, and restrooms. Many campgrounds have barrier-free sites and toilets.

Barrier-free trails include: **Fire and Ice Interpretive Trail**—0.25-mile; **Heather Meadows Artist Ridge Interpretive Trail**—0.25-mile; **Heather Meadows Picture Lake Trail**—0.5-mile; **Heather Meadows Shadow of the Sentinels Interpretive Trail**—0.5-mile; **Mountain Loop Scenic Byway Youth on Age Trail**—0.5-mile; **Mountain Loop Scenic Byway Gold Creek Pond**—0.5-mile; **Highway 90, Snoqualmie Pass Gold Basin Millpond**—0.5-mile;

Mountain Loop Scenic Byway

Children's Activities—A Junior Ranger program for children is offered in the Nooksack Valley, with a focus on Heather Meadows. A check list is available at Forest Service offices. Parents and children attend interpretive programs and walk self-guided trails to find the answers to questions on the list.

Many of the ranger-guided interpretive walks and programs are oriented toward families with children including interactive dramas, puppet shows, and living history demonstrations. Good areas for these activities are Gold

Children enjoy interpretive exhibits and ranger-guided interpretive walks at Heather Meadows, Gold Creek Pond, and other day-use areas of the national forest.
Jim Hughes, Forest Service photo.

Basin Campground on the Mountain Loop Scenic Byway, Heather Meadows on the Mount Baker Scenic Byway, and Gold Creek Pond and the Snoqualmie Pass Visitor Information Center on Interstate 90.

Forest Headquarters

Mount Baker-Snoqualmie Forest Headquarters, 21905 64th Avenue, West Mountlake Terrace, WA 98043, (206) 775-9702.

Outdoor Recreation Information Center, 915 2nd Avenue, Room 442, Seattle, WA 98174, (206) 220-7450.

Ranger District Recreation Opportunities

Mount Baker District

The Mount Baker District includes mountainous terrain from the Canadian border to just south of the Skagit River. The Nooksack and Skagit rivers are part of the district.

Information Centers

Mount Baker District Office, 2105 State Highway 20, Sedro Woolley, WA 98284, (206) 856-5700. Staffed information desk, map and book sales, interpretive exhibits, brochures and videos, permit sales, administrative center, restrooms, and pay phone. 8:00-4:30 M-F. Weekend hours vary with the seasons.

Glacier Public Service Center, State Highway 542, Glacier, WA 98244, (206) 599-2714. Staffed information desk, map and book sales, restrooms and information kiosk, indoor and outdoor interpretive exhibits, climbing register, brochures and videos, pay phone, emergency phone and radio. Hours vary with the seasons.

Heather Meadows Visitor Center, Eastern end of State Highway 542. Staffed information desk, restrooms, indoor and outdoor interpretive exhibits, interpretive trail, guided interpretive walks, emergency radio. Summer hours only.

Recreation Highlights

Heather Meadows—Located at the east end of the Mount Baker Scenic Byway. Meadows of huckleberry and heather roll for miles at the eastern end of the Mount Baker Byway. Glistening little lakes nestle among the knolls. Ridges bristle with 900-year-old mountain hemlock trees. Even the rocks at Heather Meadows catch the eye. Lava flows from Mount Baker have resisted glacial carving and stand like black anvils against the sky.

Hikers can stroll the two mile-long interpretive trails with 0.25-mile-long barrier-free sections. Exhibits along the trails explain the geology and ecology of this subalpine, volcanic environment. More ambitious hikers can stride into the Mount Baker Wilderness for long day-hikes, overnights, or mountain climbs.

Guided interpretive walks explaining natural and human history of the area are offered during the summer months by Forest Service rangers and guest specialists from the local community. Interpretive programs are given on the ski slopes in the winter when Heather Meadows becomes the Mount Baker Ski Area.

Baker Lake—Located north of State Highway 20 along the Baker Lake Highway. Baker Lake is a nine-mile-long hydro-electric reservoir north of the Skagit River. The lake provides fishing, boating, and swimming. Surrounding roads and trails provide access to the Mount Baker Wilderness and the Mount Baker Recreation Area.

The Shadow of the Sentinels Trail, located just off the Baker Lake Highway, offers a self-guided 0.5-mile interpretive walk through huge old Douglas fir trees. The entire trail is barrier-free.

Mount Baker National Recreation Area—Located on the southern slopes of Mount Baker. These 8,600 acres were set aside by Congress to preserve the unique recreational features. Most of the area can only be accessed by trails. Hiking, climbing, and snowmobiling are popular activities.

Campgrounds

North Fork Nooksack Valley

Douglas Fir—Two miles east of Glacier on Highway 542. Thirty sites and a picnic area with a picnic shelter are nestled among Douglas-fir and western hemlock trees on the bank of the Nooksack River. Open all year. 1,000 feet elevation. Fee.

Silver Fir—Fourteen miles east of Glacier on Highway 542. Twenty sites and a picnic area with a picnic shelter in an open silver fir forest along the Nooksack River. Closest campground to Heather Meadows day-use area. 2,000 feet elevation. Fee.

Skagit Valley

Horseshoe Cove—Thirty-two miles northeast of Sedro Woolley via State Highway 20 and Forest Road 11. Thirty-four sites and a picnic area in the trees on the shores of Baker Lake. A swimming beach and boat launch make this site ideal for families. 700 feet elevation. Fee.

Panorama Point—Thirty-three miles northeast of Sedro Woolley via State Highway 20 and Forest Road 11. Sixteen sites and a picnic area on the shores of Baker Lake with spectacular views of Mount Baker and Mount Shuksan. Boat launch. 700 feet elevation. Fee.

Shannon Creek—Thirty-seven miles northeast of Sedro Woolley via State Highway 20 and Forest Road 11. Twenty sites and a picnic area near the upper end of Baker Lake. Boat launch. 800 feet elevation.

Park Creek—Thirty-four miles northeast of Sedro Woolley via State Highway 20 and Forest Road 11. Twelve sites in the trees next to rushing Park Creek. Near Baker Lake. 800 feet elevation.

Boulder Creek—Thirty-two miles northeast of Sedro Woolley via State Highway 20 and Forest Road 11. Ten sites in the trees next to Boulder Creek, which flows from glaciers in Sherman Crater on the volcano, Mount Baker. 1,100 feet elevation.

Marble Creek—Eight miles up the Cascade River Road out of Marblemount on State Highway 20. Twenty-seven sites plus a picnic area located under tall trees. 1,000 feet elevation.

Heather Meadows day-use area includes the Austin Pass Picnic Area where every table has a panoramic view of surrounding peaks and glaciers.
Jim Hughes, Forest Service photo.

Mineral Park—Twenty miles up the Cascade River Road out of Marblemount on State Highway 20. Twenty-two units and a picnic area. 1,000 feet elevation.

Other Campgrounds

North Cascades National Park operates a number of developed campgrounds along State Highway 20.

Puget Power, a private utility, operates a campground at Baker Lake.

Rockport State Park and Steelhead County Park, both located at Rockport, offer camping facilities.

Resorts and Businesses

Small towns at the forest boundaries, such as Glacier and Concrete, offer food, groceries, gas, and lodging. Larger cities like Bellingham and Sedro Woolley offer a full array of services including laundromats and entertainment.

Baker Lake Resort rents cabins, campsites, and boats and has a small store. Located on the west shore of Baker Lake.

Several outfitter guides work in the Mount Baker area. Contact information centers for further information.

Bellingham Visitors Bureau, 904 Potter St., Bellingham, WA 98226. 1-800-487-2032.

Mount Vernon Chamber of Commerce, 200 E. College Way, Mount Vernon, WA 98273. (206) 428-8547.

Darrington Ranger District

The Darrington District is southeast of Mount Vernon and encompasses part of the Skagit River system, the Sauk River Valley and the Stillaguamish River. Much of the district is within the Glacier Peak Wilderness.

Information Centers

Darrington Ranger Station, 1405 Emmons St., Darrington, WA 98241, (206) 436-1155. Staffed information desk, map and book sales, permit sales, indoor and outdoor interpretive exhibits, administrative center, restrooms, pay phone. Hours vary with the seasons.

Verlot Public Service Center, Verlot, WA 98252, (206) 691-7791. Staffed information desk, map and book sales, indoor and outdoor interpretive exhibits, pit toilets, pay phone. Summer hours only.

Recreation Highlights

Big Four—Twenty-five miles east of Granite Falls via Mount Loop Scenic Byway. Six picnic sites in meadow near beaver ponds at the base of rocky crags of Big Four Mountain. A mile-long interpretive trail on boardwalks through the beaver pond interprets wetland ecology. Exhibits in picnic area interpret the history of Big Four Inn. Barrier-free restrooms.

Hemple Creek—Thirteen miles east of Granite Falls via Mountain Loop Scenic Byway. Thirty-six picnic sites in forest next to river. Fishing and hiking.

Campgrounds

Bedal— Nineteen miles southeast of Darrington via Forest Road 20. Sixteen tent sites, two picnic units, and a community picnic shelter. Fishing and whitewater rafting. Elevation 900 feet.

Clear Creek—Three miles southeast of Darrington on Forest Road 20. Seven tent or trailer sites. One picnic site. Fishing and hiking. Elevation 600 feet.

Gold Basin—Thirteen miles east of Granite Falls via Mountain Loop Scenic Byway. Ten tent sites and eighty-four tent/trailer units in forested setting. Drinking water, flush toilets, interpretive trail, and amphitheater for interpretive programs. Fishing, hiking. Elevation 1,100 feet. Fee.

Red Bridge—Eighteen miles east of Granite Falls via Mountain Loop Scenic Byway. Two tent sites and fourteen tent/trailer units in forest near river. Fishing. Elevation 1,300 feet.

Turlo—Eleven miles east of Granite Falls via Mountain Loop Scenic Byway. Nineteen tent/trailer units along the Stillaguamish River. Drinking water. Elevation 900 feet. Fee.

Verlot—Eleven miles east of Granite Falls via Mountain Loop Scenic Byway. Twenty-six tent/trailer sites in forest along river. Drinking water. Elevation 900 feet. Fee.

Resorts and Businesses

Darrington and Granite Falls offer restaurants, gas, groceries, lodging, and laundromat. Verlot offers a small store with groceries and sundries and a restaurant.

Gold Basin Campground in the Darrington Ranger District offers camping near the Stillaguamish River and access to interpretive trails, campfire programs, hiking trails and scenic drives. Wendy Walker photo.

Darrington Chamber of Commerce, P.O. Box 351, Darrington, WA 98241. (206) 436-1177.

Skykomish Ranger District

The Skykomish District lies east of Everett and includes the Skykomish River Valley and the mountains west of Stevens Pass.

Information Centers

Skykomish Ranger Station, 74920 N.E. Stevens Pass Highway, P.O. Box 305, Skykomish, WA 98288, (206) 677-2414. Staffed information desk, map and book sales, and restrooms. Monday through Friday 8-4:30. Other hours vary with seasons.

Recreation Highlights

Deception Falls Picnic Area—Eight miles east of Skykomish on State Highway 2. Picnic sites, interpretive exhibits and interpretive trail. Mile-long trail leads through old forest along whitewater creeks. A 0.25-mile barrier-free section offers viewpoints for roaring Deception Falls. Exhibits interpret water's interaction with forest processes and railroad history.

Iron Goat Trail—*Open fall of 1993.* Eleven miles east of Skykomish via Highway 2, Old Cascade Highway and Forest Road 6710. Hiking and interpretive trail, approximately two miles long, along the historic route of the Great Northern Railway. The lower portion of the trail is barrier-free. Trail will be extended in the future.

Campgrounds

Call information center twenty-four hours in advance to reserve wheelchair accessible campsites.

Beckler River—Two miles north of Skykomish via State Highway 2 and Forest Road 65. Seven tent sites and twenty tent/trailer units. Drinking water and fishing. Fee.

Money Creek—Four miles west of Skykomish off Highway 2. Twelve tent units and thirteen tent/trailer units. Swimming, fishing, and hiking. Drinking water. Fee.

San Juan—Fourteen miles northeast of Index on County Road 65. Seven tent units and four tent/trailer units. Fishing and hiking.

Troublesome Creek—Twelve miles northeast of Index on County Road 65. Nineteen tent units and twelve tent/trailer units along with three picnic sites. Fishing, hiking, and nature trail.

Resorts and Businesses

The town of Skykomish offers food, groceries, lodging, gifts, souvenirs, and gas.

Sky Valley Chamber of Commerce, 211 E. Main, P.O. Box 38, Monroe, WA 98272. (206) 794-5488.

North Bend District

The North Bend District lies just east of Seattle and includes the Snoqualmie River Valley and mountainous terrain west of Snoqualmie Pass.

Information Centers

North Bend Ranger Station, 42404 S.E. North Bend Way North Bend, WA 98045, (206) 888-1421. Staffed information desk, map and book sales, restrooms; hours vary with seasons.

Snoqualmie Pass Visitor Center, Snoqualmie Pass, Interstate 90, (206) 434-6111. Staffed information desk, interpretive exhibits. Open all year. Days and hours vary with the season.

Recreation Highlights

Asahel Curtis—Twenty miles east of North Bend off exit 47 from Interstate 90. Picnic area along the South Fork of the Snoqualmie River. Interpretive trail, memorial, and fishing.

Lake Keechelus—Twenty-seven miles east of North Bend at exit 54 off Interstate 90. Large reservoir surrounded by mountain peaks. Fishing, boat launch, and interpretive exhibits.

Gold Creek Pond—Twenty-seven miles east of North Bend at exit 54 off Interstate 90. Former gravel pit turned into a lake and wildlife area. Barrier-free picnic area, interpretive trail, and wildlife watching.

Campgrounds

Denny Creek—Twenty miles east of North Bend at exit 47 off Interstate

90 and Forest Road 58. Twenty tent sites and seventeen tent/trailer units. Fishing, historic trail, horse riding. Fee.

Tinkham—Twelve miles east of North Bend, exit 42 off Interstate 90 and Forest Road 55. Thirteen tent sites and thirty-four tent/trailer units, handicapped restrooms. Fishing and scenery. Fee.

Resorts and Businesses

North Bend offers gas, groceries, lodging, food, and laundromat.

Snoqualmie Summit has a snack bar in the winter at the ski lodge. The pass area offers restaurants, motels, convenience stores, and gas.

North Bend Visitor Center, P.O. Box 357, North Bend, WA 98045. (206) 888-1678.

White River District

The White River District lies east of Tacoma and includes the White River Valley and the mountains just north of Mount Rainier National Park.

Information Centers

White River Ranger Station, 853 Roosevelt Ave. E., Enumclaw, WA 98022, (206) 825-6585. Staffed information desk, map and book sales, restrooms, and outdoor exhibits.

Recreation Highlights

Sun Top Lookout—Thirty-five miles southeast of Enumclaw via Mather Memorial Parkway and forest roads 73 and 7315. Seven picnic sites at restored fire lookout. Scenery, berry-picking, and interpretive programs.

John Muir Trail—Twenty-five miles southeast of Enumclaw on the Mather Memorial Parkway in the Dalles Campground. Interpretive walk through old-growth grand-fir forest.

Campgrounds

Coral Pass—Thirty-seven miles southeast of Enumclaw via Mather Memorial Parkway and Forest Road 7174. Twelve tent units. Horse riding, berry picking, hiking, and scenery.

The Dalles—Twenty-five miles southeast of Enumclaw via Mather Memorial Parkway. Ten picnic sites, nineteen tent units, and twenty-six tent/trailer units among big trees along White River. Fishing, interpretive trails, hiking. Drinking water. Fee.

Silver Springs—Thirty-one miles southeast of Enumclaw via Mather Memorial Parkway. Ten picnic sites, sixteen tent sites, and forty tent/trailer units. Fishing and hiking. Drinking water. Fee.

Evans Creek—Thirty-five miles south of Enumclaw via State Highway 165. One picnic site and twenty tent/trailer units. Off-road vehicle park, picnic shelter, forty miles of ORV trail.

Resorts and Businesses

The town of Enumclaw offers gas, groceries, lodging, restaurants, and laundromat.

The town of Greenwater has gas, groceries, and restaurants.

Enumclaw Area Chamber of Commerce, 1421 Cole St., Enumclaw, WA 98022. (206) 825-2541.□

A horse camp within the Goat Rocks Wilderness in the Naches Ranger District of the Wenatchee National Forest. Forest Service photo.

WENATCHEE NATIONAL FOREST

The Wenatchee National Forest is the largest national forest in Washington. Its 2.2 million acres encompass an astonishing diversity of climate, ecosystems, landforms, and recreational opportunities.

In the western part of the Wenatchee National Forest, Cascade Mountain glaciers hang from dark crags, and small round lakes glisten blue on mountain shoulders. Green forest aprons spread down ridges. Streams flow in valley bottoms like silver ribbons. In the more arid eastern part, forests thin until pine gives way to sagebrush and the mighty Columbia River hugs the dry brown foothills of the Cascades.

The Wenatchee National Forest contains 2,600 miles of trail, 5,000 miles of forest roads, 151 campgrounds, nine proposed Wild and Scenic Rivers, seven wilderness areas, and seven commercial ski areas. The forest records more than ten million visits each year, making it one of the most heavily-used recreation forests in the nation.

Location

The Wenatchee National Forest in central Washington shares the eastern slopes of the Cascade Mountains with the Okanogan National Forest to the north and the Yakima Indian Reservation to the south. It stretches from the Cascade Crest in the west to the Columbia River in the east.

The urban areas nearest to the national forest are Wenatchee, Ellensburg, and Yakima, small cities in eastern Washington within an hour's drive of the forest boundary. The large coastal cities of Seattle and Tacoma are within a two- to three-hour drive of the national forest via major highways over the Cascade Mountains.

Climate

Elevations vary within the national forest from 700 feet along the eastern border to over 8,000 feet along the Cascade crest. Precipitation at higher elevations usually comes in the form of snow during the winter months and averages 120 inches. In the eastern and lower portions of the national forest, precipitation averages only ten inches a year.

Most of the summer months offer sunny, clear weather except for scattered lightning storms that pass over the national forest during the afternoons in the summer months. Temperatures hover in the eighties during the day and drop to the fifties at night. The winters are cold, with some rain and snow, but much drier than the rainy west side of the Cascade Mountains.

The forest basks in sunny weather most of the time because of the rainshadow created by the Cascade Range. Wet clouds blowing in off the Pacific Ocean rise over the Cascades and drop most of their moisture on the western slopes of the mountains. Clouds east of the crest are often puffy white cumulus, wrung dry and rainless.

Geology

Most of the national forest lies in the Cascade Mountains, a very young mountain range that began rising just six million years ago. The mountains

WENATCHEE NATIONAL FOREST

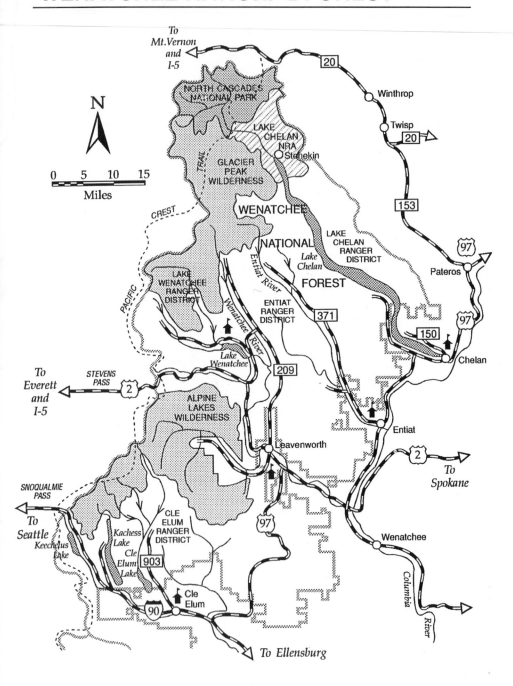

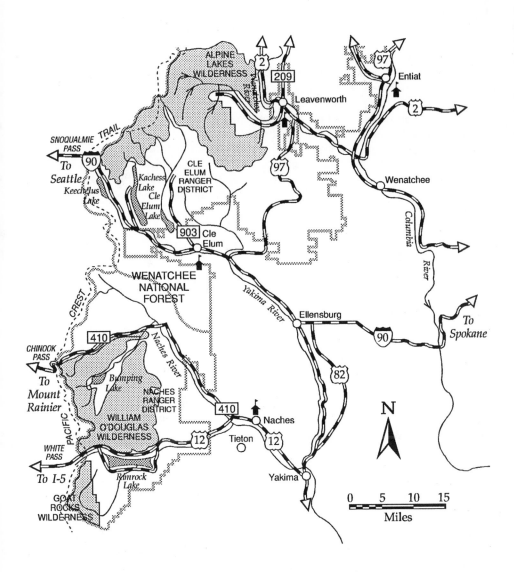

ALPINE LAKES WILDERNESS

To Seattle

SNOQUALMIE PASS

TRAIL

90

Keechelus Lake

Kachess Lake

Cle Elum Lake

903 Cle Elum

CLE ELUM RANGER DISTRICT

WENATCHEE NATIONAL FOREST

2

209

Leavenworth

97

97

Entiat

2

Wenatchee

Columbia River

Yakima River

Ellensburg

90

To Spokane

CREST

PACIFIC

410

Bumping Lake

NACHES RANGER DISTRICT

WILLIAM O'DOUGLAS WILDERNESS

CHINOOK PASS

To Mount Rainier

WHITE PASS

To I-5

Rimrock Lake

GOAT ROCKS WILDERNESS

Naches River

410

Naches

12

Tieton

12

82

Yakima

N

0   5   10   15
Miles

formed because of a crumpling of the edge of North America as it floated westward and ran aground on the eastward-moving Pacific Ocean floor. The mountains are still rising today, at about the same rate as your fingernails are growing.

The volcanos in the Cascades, like Glacier Peak, resulted from melting of the ocean floor as it sank beneath the continent. The melted rock rose through cracks in the continent to erupt as lava formed the Cascade volcanos. This process of recycling the ocean floor continues today, accounting for the eruption of Mount St. Helens and steam vents and hot springs in the other dormant volcanos.

Eastern Washington is a broad lava plateau formed from immense, long-term eruptions of liquid basalt from cracks in the ground many millions of years ago. Layers and layers of lava form the Columbia Plateau. The Columbia River cuts its way through the plateau at the eastern edge of the national forest.

Ecology

Distribution of precipitation over the thirty-mile width of the national forest creates striking differences between ecosystems in various parts of the forest. Mountain meadows at the crest of the Cascades receive enough precipitation to support wildflowers and trees. The slopes below are wet enough for pine forests, but the rolling hills near the Columbia River are so dry they only support sagebrush and jackrabbits.

Some ecosystems host mountain goats and marmots while others are home to rattlesnakes and lizards. An old clearcut overgrown with brush may be habitat for elk while a thick forest nearby may be home to spotted owls and flying squirrels.

Fire was a natural part of most of the ecosystems of the Wenatchee National Forest for thousands of years until modern humans began suppressing fire. In the past, fire swept through the dry pine forests of the forest every ten or twenty years, burning away trees and debris and starting the forest over again with vigorous young growth. Some organisms such as Thompson's clover and lodgepole pine are especially dependent on fire for their vitality. Today, some forests are becoming unhealthy stands of decaying trees due to lack of regular burning.

History

The area we now call the Wenatchee National Forest was home for several different groups of Indians for many thousands of years. Tribes fished, hunted, and found spiritual renewal in the mountains and valleys of the eastern Cascades. Modern tribes such as the Yakima Nation retain treaty rights to some uses of the national forest.

The first non-Indian explorers were looking for furs, gold, or railroad routes over the rugged Cascade Mountains and often traveled the traditional Indian trails in their journeys. Homesteaders and ranchers followed on the heels of these early explorers and much of the arable land became private property.

People used the national forest for grazing their cattle, harvesting wood products, and prospecting for gold and other minerals. Mining was profitable in some places, especially around the Holden area just west of Lake Chelan. The Holden mine was the largest mine in Washington State until it closed in the early 1950s.

The Forest Service began managing these public lands in 1905. The agency has evolved over the last century from caretakers to active managers of forest resources. Timber harvest, mining, and grazing dominated the national forest for decades in the twentieth century until recent years when recreation uses of the forest began to dominate.

Forest-wide Recreation Opportunities

Scenic Drives

The 4,700 miles of forest roads wind through a variety of scenery from high meadows and mountains to forested river bottoms. Scenic drives vary with the seasons, offering snowy vistas in the early spring, wildflowers in the summer, and bright leaves in the autumn. Most forest roads are closed by snow from November to April.

The mountain passes within the national forest are especially scenic and are accessed by paved multi-lane highways. Blewett Pass on Highway 97, Snoqualmie Pass on Interstate 90, and Stevens Pass on Highway 2 are beautiful drives.

Additional examples of enjoyable scenic drives include:

Entiat River Road—This river-bottom drive along Forest Road 51 is especially beautiful during the fall colors. The river runs clear, cottonwood and aspen trees glow yellow along the river banks, and sumac and Douglas maples color the hillsides with oranges and reds.

Tumwater Canyon—Highway 2, a paved two-lane road between Wenatchee and Everett, winds next to the Wenatchee River west of Leavenworth. The river is confined by the Tumwater Canyon walls and is a raging torrent, especially worth seeing and hearing during spring runoff.

Wilderness Areas

Lake Chelan-Sawtooth Wilderness—56,456 acres in the Wenatchee National Forest contain rocky canyons, jagged peaks, and large wildflower meadows.

Glacier Peak Wilderness—289,234 acres in the Wenatchee National Forest have numerous active glaciers and Glacier Peak, a dormant volcano 10,541 feet high. Accessed from the north and south by the Pacific Crest National Scenic Trail.

Henry M. Jackson Wilderness—27,242 acres in the Wenatchee National Forest include easy day hikes to mountain lakes as well as part of the Pacific Crest National Scenic Trail north of Stevens Pass.

Alpine Lakes Wilderness—246,330 acres in the Wenatchee National Forest include 800 miles of trail over a landscape dotted with hundreds of small mountain lakes. Permits required for Enchantments area near Leavenworth.

Norse Peak Wilderness—51,364 acres in the Wenatchee National Forest straddle the crest of the Cascade Mountains between Chinook and Naches passes. Near Mount Rainier.

William O. Douglas Wilderness—152,408 acres in the Wenatchee National Forest include hundreds of small lakes and tributaries for four major rivers.

Goat Rocks Wilderness—36,333 acres in the Wenatchee National Forest include many volcanic features. Mountain goats can sometimes be seen near Bear Creek Mountain.

Special Areas

Stevens Pass Historic District—In the Leavenworth District near Stevens Pass on Highway 2, this historic area was the route of the Great Northern Railway built in the 1890s to connect Puget Sound with the outside world by rail. The historic district commemorates the astounding engineering of this early railway.

Wildlife

A wide variety of animals, birds, and fish make the Wenatchee National Forest their home. The diversity of climate and ecosystems also allows for a wide diversity of species.

Early morning and late evening are the best times to spot large mammals. Some common species include: mule deer, elk, black bear, beaver, porcupine, hoary marmot, chipmunk, squirrel, and jackrabbit. Less common mammals include mountain goat, moose, coyote, mountain lion, and bobcat. Rare and endangered mammals include: gray wolf and grizzly bear.

Amphibians and reptiles found in the national forest include: rubber boa, western rattlesnake, common garter snake, western skink, long-toed salamander, tailed frog, and Pacific giant salamander.

Migratory birds come from all over the Western Hemisphere to use the Wenatchee National Forest for parts of their life cycles. Resident birds live in the forest all year, sometimes migrating to lower elevations in the winter. Common species include hummingbird, great blue heron, mallard duck, wood duck, Canadian geese, red-tailed hawk, varied thrush, robin, Swainson's thrush, brown creeper, common raven, Steller's jay, and dark-eyed juncoe. Rare and endangered birds include northern spotted owl, American peregrine falcon, and bald eagle.

Fish found within national forest waters include white sturgeon, prickly sculpin, common carp, bluegill, salmon, whitefish, dace, and many species of trout.

Hunting

The Wenatchee National Forest is known throughout the state for fine elk hunting. Hunters also stalk mule deer, black bear, and upland birds. Washington State game laws apply.

Fishing

Two hundred and forty-one lakes and reservoirs and 1,769 miles of streams and rivers offer outstanding fishing opportunities. Game fish include coho, sockeye and kokanee salmon, several varieties of trout, burbot, smallmouth bass, largemouth bass, and yellow perch. Some species are endangered such as bulltrout, or dolly varden, and are protected from fishing in most of their habitat areas. Washington State fishing regulations apply.

Gentle water on the lower stretches of the White River offers ideal canoe trips in the Wenatchee National Forest. Forest Service photo.

Foraging

Berries can be found in the western parts of the national forest from mid- to late summer. Berries are best in subalpine meadows and in cleared areas near forests. Bears like berries as much as people, so pickers should make noise to avoid startling a bear.

Mushrooms are most plentiful during the fall months and are found in greatest numbers in forested valleys, especially along rivers or streams. No permit is needed for home use, but commercial harvesters must purchase a permit from a Forest Service office.

Firewood can be gathered for campground use. A low-cost permit is available for cutting a few cords of firewood for home use. Commercial firewood cutters need a special permit. Permits are issued at most Forest Service offices.

Christmas tree permits are sold each November and December for visitors who want the experience of cutting their own tree. Special cutting areas are designated.

Water Recreation

Rivers offering whitewater canoeing, kayaking, and rafting include the Wenatchee, White, and Tieton. Rushing water, rocks, and logs require expert skills or experienced guides. Rivers are especially dangerous when swollen with melting snow during May and June.

Winter Recreation

Downhill Skiing

Mission Ridge Ski Area–four chairlifts and two rope tows. Thirteen miles from Wenatchee.

Stevens Pass Ski Area–eight chairlifts. Thirty-five miles east of Leavenworth.

Snoqualmie Summit–twenty-two lifts spread across four ski areas. Fifty miles east of Seattle.

White Pass Ski Area–four chairlifts and one rope tow. Sixteen miles east of Packwood.

Cross-country Skiing and Snowshoeing

The national forest has 120 miles of maintained, signed ski and snowshoe trails. Skiers also use snow-covered roads and open terrain. Avalanches pose dangers at higher elevations in the Cascades during the winter months. A good trip for beginners or families might be: **Squirrel Run Ski Trail**—Lake Wenatchee District, Chiwawa Sno Park. Easy rolling trip through forest along the base of a ridge above County Road 22. Four miles roundtrip.

Snowmobiling

Thousands of miles of forest roads are available each winter along with 450 miles of groomed snowmobile trails.

Snowplay

The only formal snowplay area is "Wintertube" located at Snoqualmie Pass on Interstate 90, but the snow-covered forest offers ample opportunities for informal snowplay areas along every forest road.

SnoParks

These are designated plowed parking locations adjacent to winter sports areas. Washington State Parks uses permit funds to plow parking areas and groom ski and snowmobile trails. Vehicles parked in these lots without permits may be ticketed. Permits can be purchased at ski shops and stores and are also valid in Oregon and Idaho.

Off-road Vehicles

All national forest roads are available for four-wheel-drive vehicles and motorcycles. Nearly 800 miles of trail are open to motorbikes and mountain bikes.

Information centers offer complete listings of trails open to off-road vehicles. The following trails are just examples:

Naches District—Mud Spring, 4.2 miles; Milk Creek, 2.2 miles; and Clover Spring, 3.1 miles. Lake Wenatchee District—Alder Ridge, 4.0 miles; and Minnow Ridge, 2.6 miles.

Mountain Bikes

Mountain bike trails in the forest include: Naches District—Pyramid Peak, 7.1 miles; Mount Clifty, 5.6 miles, more difficult; and Spencer Creek, 2.2 miles. Lake Wenatchee District—Dirty Face, 4.5 miles; and South Shore, 1.2 miles.

Backcountry Travel

Hikers and horses use more than 2,600 miles of trails, forty-eight percent of which are within wilderness areas. The Pacific Crest National Scenic Trail runs the north-south length of the national forest near the crest of the Cascade Mountains. This trail passes through spectacular alpine scenery within six wilderness areas. A total of 153 miles of the 2,500-mile Mexico-to-Canada route are within the Wenatchee National Forest. The trail is open to stock but closed to wheeled and motorized vehicles.

Excellent trail guides are available for hiking in the national forest. The following are just a few examples of the many opportunities.

Non-wilderness Trails

Round Mountain—Lake Wenatchee District. Trailhead located at the end of Forest Road 6910 off Highway 2. Four-and-a-half miles to Alpine Lookout. Moderate grade. No water. Open to hikers, mountain bikers, and stock.

Lake Creek—Entiat District. Trailhead located off Forest Road 51, the Entiat River Road. Ten-and-a-half miles from Entiat Valley to Devils Backbone Trail. Open to hikers, stock, and mountain bikes.

Wilderness Trails

Heather Lake—Lake Wenatchee District. Trailhead located at the end of Forest Road 400 via Forest Road 6701. Three-and-a-half miles at moderate grades to lake at 4,000 feet. Possible hazardous crossing of Lake Creek early in season. Hikers only.

Emerald Park—Entiat District. Trailhead located at the end of Forest Road 51. The connecting trail between the Entiat Valley and upper Lake Chelan. Steep and rocky in places. Spectacular views from snowslide meadows along Snowbrushy Creek. Five miles of hiking along the Entiat River and then five more miles up to Milham Pass, one way.

Horse Trails

There are 2,200 miles of trails in the national forest open to stock. Several outfitter/guides offer commercial pack trips into the national forest. Contact ranger stations for addresses and phone numbers.

Mountain Climbing

The granite rocks of the Leavenworth District of the Wenatchee National Forest are famous statewide for their rock climbing opportunities. Climbers are especially drawn to peaks in the Enchantments, but permits are required for entering this highly popular backcountry area.

Snow climbers can ascend glacier-smothered Glacier Peak at the center of the Glacier Peak Wilderness as well as the snowfields and glaciers of hundreds of other Cascade Mountain peaks.

Most Cascade climbs require special equipment and experience or guides. Rock and snow climbers should be well-booted and always carry climbing ropes. Snow climbers also should carry ice axes and crampons all year. All climbers should be prepared for emergencies with extra food and clothing and first aid supplies.

Excellent climbing guides have been published for the Cascades and can be purchased at most area bookstores and some Forest Service information stations.

Barrier-free Sites

All information stations and most campgrounds and restrooms offer barrier-free access.

Children's Activities

Children may enjoy the commercial boat ride up fifty-five-mile-long Lake Chelan on the Lady of the Lake passenger ferry. Take along coloring books or toys in case the ride gets a little long. Families may want to consider taking the fast boat rather than the slower boat. The boat docks in Stehekin, within North Cascades National Park, for an hour or two at lunch time. Stehekin offers swimming, bike rentals, restaurants, visitor center exhibits, and programs that would interest children.

The interpretive programs offered by Leavenworth District interpreters in downtown Leavenworth are often oriented toward families and children. One program includes an interpreter dressed up as an old-time miner accompanied by a live mule.

Children's programs are offered in some campgrounds during the summer months. These typically involve an hour or two in the morning. Parents are welcome to attend as well.

An interpretive drive up the White River Road in the Lake Wenatchee District offers interpretive stops at features of historic and natural interest. A brochure is available at the Lake Wenatchee Ranger Station.

Boulder Cave in the Naches District offers kids a chance to explore the mouth of this lava cave just off Highway 410 and maybe see bats in the late evening.

Forest Headquarters

Wenatchee National Forest Headquarters, 301 Yakima St., P.O. Box 811, Wenatchee, WA 98807. (509) 662-4335.

Ranger District Recreation Opportunities

Chelan Ranger District

Information Centers

Chelan Ranger Station, 428 Woodin Ave., P.O. Box 189, Chelan, WA 98816, (509) 682-2576. Staffed information desk, map and book sales. Joint Forest Service/Park Service information center. Permits for Lake Chelan National Recreation Area.

Cub lake glistens within the roadless high country in the Chelan Ranger District. The lake is accessible to hikers, horse users, motorbikers, and mountain bikers.
Forest Service photo.

Recreation Highlights

Lake Chelan—This fifty-five-mile-long lake fills a 1,600-foot-deep basin dug by ice-age glaciers. Lake Chelan is the third-deepest lake in the United States after Crater Lake and Lake Tahoe. Roads access the lower third of the lake, but the upper sections can only be reached by boat, plane, or trail. Boat camps dot the lakeshore. Waterfalls and rugged mountain peaks provide a backdrop for the clear, shimmering waters of the lake. A passenger ferry service runs up and down the lake from Chelan to Stehekin once a day during the late spring, summer, early fall, and two to three times a week during the winter months.

Fields Point—Large day-use facility with visitor information center. Located at the passenger ferry dock on the south shore of Lake Chelan. The ferry may be boarded here or in the town of Chelan. Picnic sites, parking, food, and barrier-free trail.

Campgrounds

Ramona Park—Twenty-three miles northwest of Chelan. Eight tent units. Hiking and motorbiking. Elevation 1,900 feet.

South Navarre—Thirty-three miles northwest of Chelan via State Highway 150 and Forest Road 8200. Four tent units. Stock facilities, hiking, and scenery. Elevation 6,000 feet.

Lucerne—Forty-one miles northwest of Chelan via Lake Chelan, boat, hiking, horse, or plane. Two lakeside tent units. Boating, swimming, fishing, waterskiing, and hiking. Elevation 1,100 feet.

Prince Creek—Thirty-five miles northwest of Chelan via Lake Chelan, boat, hiking, horse, or plane. Six lakeside tent units. Boating, swimming, fishing, waterskiing, and hiking. Elevation 1,100 feet.

Safety Harbor—Twenty-six miles northwest of Chelan via Lake Chelan, boat, or plane. Two tent units. Boating, swimming, fishing, and waterskiing. Elevation 1,100 feet.

Moore Point—Six miles south of Stehekin via Lake Chelan, boat, plane, horse, or hiking. One shelter and four tent units. Boating, swimming, fishing, waterskiing, and hiking. Elevation 1,100 feet.

Big Creek—Twenty-six miles northwest of Chelan via Lake Chelan, boat, or plane. Four tent sites. Boating, swimming, and a shelter. Elevation 1,100 feet.

Deer Point—Twenty-two miles northwest of Chelan via Lake Chelan, boat, or plane. Four tent sites. Boating, fishing, swimming, and waterskiing. Elevation 1,100 feet.

Mitchell Creek—Sixteen miles northwest of Chelan via Lake Chelan, boat, or plane. One shelter and six tent units. Boating, swimming, fishing, and waterskiing. Elevation 1,100 feet.

Refrigerator Harbor—Forty miles northwest of Chelan via Lake Chelan, boat, or plane. Four tent sites. Boating, hiking, fishing, waterskiing, and swimming. Elevation 1,100 feet.

Domke Lake—Thirty-six miles northwest of Chelan via Lake Chelan, float plane, or trail. Eight tent sites. Boat and cabin rental, hiking, and fishing. Elevation 2,200 feet.

Domke Falls—Thirty-eight miles northwest of Chelan via Lake Chelan, boat, or plane. Three tent sites. Boating, swimming, fishing, and waterskiing. Elevation 1,100 feet.

Holden—Thirty-six miles northwest of Chelan via Lake Chelan and Forest Road 8301 (accessible only by boat or plane). Two tent sites and Forest Service guard station. Hiking, historic mining town operated as a private retreat center, and entry to Glacier Peak Wilderness. Elevation 3,200 feet.

Graham Harbor—Thirty-one miles northwest of Chelan via Lake Chelan, boat, or plane. Four tent sites and shelter. Boating and swimming. Elevation 1,100 feet.

Antilon Lake—Eighteen miles from Chelan on the north shore of Lake Chelan. Dispersed camping with some fishing. Elevation 2,400 feet.

Jr. Point—Thirty-two miles from Chelan on the south shore off Forest Road 5900. Excellent view from old lookout site. Five tent sites. Elevation 6,600 feet.

Grouse Mountain and Grouse Mountain Springs—Twenty-six miles from Chelan off Forest Road 5900. Five tent sites. Elevation 4,400 feet.

Handy Springs—Thirty-four miles from Chelan off Forest Road 5900. One tent site. Elevation 6,400 feet.

Poison Springs—North shore of Lake Chelan off Forest Road 8200. One primitive tent site, remotely located. Elevation 5,800 feet.

Other Campgrounds and Facilities

Lakeshore City Park—Offers overnight camping with 161 sites, swimming beach, and picnic area. Downtown Chelan. No tents during summer months.

Lake Chelan State Park—Camping and picnicking on the south shore of Lake Chelan. One hundred forty-four sites with seventeen full hook-ups. Swimming, boat launch, store, and showers. Reservations required during summer.

Twenty-Five Mile Creek State Park—Camping and picnicking on the lakeshore at the end of road access south shore of Lake Chelan. Seventy-seven sites with some hookups. Store, marine gas, boat launch, moorage, and swimming.

Entiat Ranger District

Information Centers

Entiat Ranger Station, 2108 Entiat Way, P.O. Box 476, Entiat, WA 98822, (509) 784-1511. Staffed information desk, map, and restrooms.

Recreation Highlights

Silver Falls Trail—Steep trail up to the base of spectacular 120-foot-high Silver Falls. Trail continues climbing alongside the falls, crosses above it and then descends on the other side forming a one-mile loop. Trailhead located at Silver Falls Campground off Forest Road 51.

Campgrounds

Pine Flat—Fifteen miles northwest of Entiat via County Road 371 and Forest Road 5700. Five tent sites and a twenty-person group reservation site. Fishing, riding, motorcycle trails, and horses. Elevation 1,900 feet.

Fox Creek—Twenty-eight miles northwest of Entiat via County Road 371 and Forest Road 51. Sixteen tent/trailer units and drinking water. Fishing. Elevation 2,300 feet. Fee.

Lake Creek—Thirty miles northwest of Entiat via County Road 371 and Forest Road 51. Seventeen tent/trailer units, one picnic site, and drinking water. Fishing and trails. Elevation 2,400 feet. Fee.

Silver Falls—Thirty-two miles northwest of Entiat via County Road 371 and Forest Road 51. Three picnic sites, thirty-one tent/trailer units, and a thirty-person group reservation site. Drinking water. Fishing, big trees, waterfall, and interpretive trail. Elevation 2,400 feet. Fee.

North Fork—Thirty-five miles northwest of Entiat via County Road 371 and Forest Road 51. Eight tent/trailer units. Drinking water. Fishing. Elevation 2,700 feet. Fee.

Cottonwood—Thirty-nine miles northwest of Entiat via County Road 371 and Forest Road 51. Twenty five tent/trailer units. Drinking water. Trails and berry picking. Elevation 3,100 feet. Fee.

Spruce Grove—Thirty-seven miles northwest of Entiat via County Road 371 and Forest Road 51. Two tent/trailer units by the Entiat River. Fishing. Elevation 2,900 feet.

The Entiat River rushes through evergreen forests on its journey from mountain glaciers to the Columbia River. Forest Service photo.

Three Creek—Thirty-eight miles from Entiat via County Road 371 and Forest Road 51. Three tent/trailer units. Elevation 2,900 feet.

Other Campgrounds and Facilities
Entiat City Park—Campsites and picnic area. Swimming.

Resorts and Businesses
The small town of Entiat offers groceries and gas.

Lake Wenatchee Ranger District

Information Centers
Lake Wenatchee Ranger Station, 22976 Highway 207, Leavenworth, WA 98826, (509) 763-3103. Staffed information desk, map and book sales, and restrooms.

Recreation Highlights
Nason Creek and Bygone Byways Interpretive Trail—Railroad history comes alive at these interpretive exhibits along a short trail just off Highway 2 east of Stevens Pass within the Stevens Pass Historic District. Signs and a brochure tell the story of the Great Northern Railway's pioneer route over the Cascades, built in the 1890s.

Lake Wenatchee—A large tree-rimmed lake offering boating, swimming, waterskiing, and fishing. Hiking, riding, biking, and off-road vehicle trails are located nearby. Forest Service campgrounds, a state park campground, boat launch, and private lodging available.

Campgrounds
Nason Creek—Nineteen miles northwest of Leavenworth via U.S. Highway 2 and State Highway 207. Twenty tent units, fifty-six tent/trailer units, and drinking water. Boating, swimming, horseback riding, and waterskiing. Showers available at adjacent state park. Elevation 1,800 feet. Fee.

Glacier View—Twenty-five miles northwest of Leavenworth via U.S. Highway 2, State Highway 207 and Forest Road 6607. Twenty tent units. Drinking water, boating, swimming, fishing, hiking, and waterskiing. Elevation 1,900 feet. Fee.

Soda Springs—Thirty-three miles northwest of Leavenworth via U.S. Highway 2, State Highway 207, and Forest Road 6500. Eight tent units. Berry picking, fishing, and nature trails. Elevation 2,000 feet.

Lake Creek—Thirty-six miles northwest of Leavenworth via U.S. Highway 2, State Highway 207, and Forest Road 6500. Eight tent sites. Fishing and berry picking. Elevation 2,300 feet.

Little Wenatchee Ford—Forty miles northwest of Leavenworth via U.S. Highway 2, State Highway 207, and Forest Road 6500. Three tent units. Fishing, berry picking, and entrance to the Glacier Peak Wilderness. Access for Pacific Crest Trail. Stock ramps and hitching rails. Elevation 2,900 feet.

Theseus Creek—Thirty-six miles northwest of Leavenworth via U.S. Highway 2, Highway 207, and forest roads 6500 and 6701. Two campsites. Fishing and berry picking. Elevation 2,200 feet.

Anglers of all ages enjoy fishing the Wenatchee River. Forest Service photo.

White River Falls—Thirty-four miles northwest of Leavenworth via U.S. Highway 2, State Highway 207, and Forest Road 6400. Five tent sites. Fishing and entrance to Glacier Peak Wilderness. Impressive but dangerous waterfall. Elevation 2,100 feet.

Grasshopper Meadows—Thirty-three miles northwest of Leavenworth via U.S. Highway 2, Highway 207, and Forest Road 6400. Four tent units. Fishing. Elevation 2,050 feet.

Napeequa—Thirty-one miles northwest of Leavenworth via U.S. Highway 2, State Highway 207, and Forest Road 6400. Three tent units and two tent/trailer units. Entrance to Glacier Peak Wilderness. Fishing and hiking. Elevation 2,000 feet.

Goose Creek—Twenty-one miles north of Leavenworth via U.S. Highway 2, Highway 207, County Road 22, and Forest Road 6200. Thirty-two tent/trailer units, accessible toilets, and drinking water. Access to motorcycle trails. Elevation 2,200 feet. Fee.

Chiwawa Horse Camp—Thirty-two miles northwest of Leavenworth via U.S. Highway 2, State Highway 207, County Road 22, and forest roads 62 and 6200. Twenty-one tent/trailer sites. Horse ramps, hitching rails, water troughs, drinking water, accessible toilets, and access to horse trails. Elevation 2,500 feet. Fee after 1994.

Alder Creek—Twenty-one miles northwest of Leavenworth via U.S. Highway 2, Highway 207, County Road 22, and forest roads 62 and 6200. Four tent/trailer sites. Horse ramps, corral, hitching rails, access to horse trails. Elevation 2,400 feet.

Grouse Creek—Twenty-five miles northwest of Leavenworth via U.S. Highway 2, Highway 207, County Road 22, and forest roads 62 and 6200. Group reservation site for up to seventy-five people. No water. Hiking and berry picking. Elevation 2,400 feet.

Finner Creek—Northwest of Leavenworth via U.S. Highway 2, Highway 207, County Road 22, and forest roads 62 and 6200. Three tent units. Drinking water, hiking. Campground hosts. Elevation 2,500 feet.

Dispersed Camping along Chiwawa River—Five small non-fee campgrounds are available past Finner Creek. Fishing. Elevations around 2,500 feet.

Phelps Creek—Forty-two miles northwest of Leavenworth via State Highway 207, County Road 22, and forest roads 62 and 6200. Seven tent units. Horse ramps and trails. Access to Glacier Peak Wilderness. Elevation 2,800 feet.

Whitepine—Twenty-five miles northwest of Leavenworth via U.S. Highway 2. Four tent sites. Fishing and berry picking. Elevation 1,900 feet.

Other Campgrounds

Lake Wenatchee State Park—Nineteen miles northwest of Leavenworth via U.S. Highway 2 and State Highway 207. One hundred ninety-two campsites and group camp. Swimming, boating, waterskiing, fishing, hiking, showers, drinking water, cross-country skiing, snowmobiling. Elevation 1,900 feet. Fee.

Resorts and Businesses

Private resorts at the lake offer groceries, gas, year-round camping, motel rooms, cabin rentals, horseback riding, hiking, cross-country skiing, water skiing, canoeing, river rafting, snowmobiling, windsurfing, swimming, fishing, biking, golf, boating, hunting, and tennis. Contact **Leavenworth Chamber of Commerce** for more information: (509) 548-5807.

Leavenworth Ranger District

Information Centers

Leavenworth Ranger Station, 600 Sherbourne St., Leavenworth, WA 98826, (509) 782-1413. Staffed information desk, map and book sales, and restrooms.

Recreation Highlights

Tumwater Canyon—Steep-sided rocky gorge of the Wenatchee River. The river roars through the canyon in an impressive series of violent rapids. Highway 2 winds alongside the river, offering turnouts for viewing and hearing the wild river.

Icicle Creek Road—Scenic road along a tributary to the Wenatchee River. Provides access to campgrounds and trails leading into the Alpine Lakes Wilderness and popular Enchantments. Permits required for hiking into the Enchantments area of the wilderness.

Leavenworth Interpretive Programs—Interpretive walks in Leavenworth and presentations at Tumwater Campground during the summer. Presentations may include gold panning demonstrations, mining history, Indian legends, or railroad history. Interpretive walks may include plant identification. Contact Leavenworth Ranger Station for schedule.

The Wenatchee River runs through Tumwater Canyon near Leavenworth, Washington. Highway 2 winds alongside the river within the canyon. Forest Service photo.

Campgrounds

Eightmile—Eight miles southwest of Leavenworth on Forest Road 7600. Forty-five units. Handicapped-accessible vault toilets, garbage service. One group site, reservations required. Fishing and hiking. Elevation 1,800 feet. Fee.

Bridge Creek—Nine miles southwest of Leavenworth on Forest Road 7600. Six tent units, trailers to nineteen feet. Drinking water, vault toilets, and garbage service. Fishing and hiking. Elevation 1,900 feet. Fee. One primitive group site, reservations required, provide own toilet and water.

Upper and Lower Johnny Creek—Twelve miles west of Leavenworth on Forest Road 7600. Eight walk-in tent units, sixty-five tent/trailer units, handicapped-accessible vault toilets, garbage service, and drinking water. Fishing and trails. Elevation 2,300 feet. Fee.

Ida Creek—Fourteen miles west of Leavenworth on Forest Road 7600. Five tent units, five tent/trailer units. Handicapped-accessible vault toilets, garbage service. Fishing and hiking. Elevation 1,900 feet. Fee.

Chatter Creek—Sixteen miles west of Leavenworth on Forest Road 7600. Nine tent sites, three tent/trailer units. Vault toilets, garbage service, and drinking water. One group site by reservation. Fishing and hiking. Elevation 2,800 feet. Fee.

Rock Island—Seventeen miles west of Leavenworth on Forest Road 7600. Twelve tent units, ten tent/trailer units. Handicapped-accessible vault toilets, garbage service, and drinking water. Fishing and hiking. Elevation 2,900 feet. Fee.

Blackpine Creek Horse Camp—Eighteen miles west of Leavenworth on Forest Road 7700. Six tent units, two tent/trailer units. Vault toilets, garbage service, stock ramp, and drinking water. Fishing and trails. Elevation 3,000 feet. Fee.

Tumwater—Ten miles northwest of Leavenworth via U.S. Highway 2. Five picnic units, eighty-four tent/trailer units, handicapped-accessible toilets, garbage service, and drinking water. One group site with shelter and fireplace, by reservation. Fishing and trails. Elevation 2,000 feet. Fee.

Tronsen—*CLOSED FOR REHABILITATION UNTIL 1995.* Twenty-three miles south of Leavenworth via U.S. Highway 2 and U.S. Highway 97. Two picnic sites, thirteen tent units and twelve tent/trailer units. Drinking water. Trails and picnicking. Elevation 3,900 feet. Fee.

Other Campgrounds

Blu-Shastin RV Park—3300 State Highway 97, Leavenworth, (509) 548-4184. Fee.

Chalet RV Park—Highway 2 and Duncan Road, Leavenworth, (509) 548-4578. Fee.

Icicle River RV Park and Campground—7305 Icicle Creek Road, Leavenworth, (509) 548-5420. Fee.

Pine Village KOA Kampground—11401 River Bend Drive, Leavenworth, (509) 548-7709. Fee.

Resorts and Businesses

The town of Leavenworth offers a full range of services and a downtown remodeled to resemble a Bavarian village with arts and crafts and other gift stores.

A peaceful afternoon for fishing on the Icicle River within the Leavenworth District of Wenatchee National Forest. Forest Service photo.

Cle Elum Ranger District

Information Centers

Cle Elum Ranger Station, 803 W. 2nd St., Cle Elum, WA 98922, (509) 674-4411. Staffed information desk, map and book sales, and restrooms.

Recreation Highlights

Kachess Lake—This large reservoir with 4,500 acres of water near Snoqualmie Pass offers boating (ten mph speed limit), fishing and swimming, views of surrounding peaks, waterskiing, berry picking, and photography. Large campground set in old-growth forest on the northwest shore of the lake.

Cle Elum Lake—This large reservoir near Cle Elum, offers boating, fishing, swimming, hiking, berry-picking, and photography.

Alpine Lakes Wilderness—Trail access into wild mountainous areas with sheer granite peaks and crystal clear mountain lakes.

Snoqualmie Pass Ski Areas—Downhill skiing and groomed cross-country ski trails during the winter months.

Swauk Forest Discovery Trail—This interpretive trail is located at the top of Swauk/Blewett Pass on Highway 97. The trail guides visitors past many examples of forest management.

John Wayne/Iron Horse Trail—Sixteen miles of this cross-state trail traverse the district. Open all year for hiking, horseback riding, cross-country skiing and snowshoeing. Access is from Interstate 90, exit 54 and then south on the Keechelus boat launch road about one mile to trailhead. Tunnels along this old railroad grade are closed because of safety.

Campgrounds

Crystal Springs—Twenty-one miles northwest of Cle Elum via Interstate 90 and Forest Road 54. Five picnic units, twenty tent sites, ten tent/trailer units, community kitchen, and drinking water. Berries, mushrooms, fishing. Elevation 2,400 feet. Fee.

Kachess—Twenty-six miles northwest of Cle Elum via Interstate 90 and Forest Road 49. Thirty-four picnic units, ninety-one tent sites, ninety-one tent/trailer units, group site, and drinking water. Forty-one reservable sites through the Mistix Reservation System, 1-800-283-CAMP. Water sports, boat launch, lake, interpretive trail and hiking. Elevation 2,300 feet. Fee.

Cle Elum River—Eighteen miles northwest of Cle Elum on County Road 903. Two tent units, thirty-three tent/trailer units, small group sites, and drinking water. Fishing. Elevation 2,200 feet. Fee.

Red Mountain—Twenty miles northwest of Cle Elum on County Road 903. Two tent units, small group sites, and thirteen tent/trailer units. Fishing. Elevation 2,300 feet.

Salmon La Sac—Twenty-two miles northwest of Cle Elum on County Road 903. Eleven picnic sites, thirty tent sites, eighty tent/trailer sites, fifteen-unit horse camp, community kitchen, and drinking water. Twenty-seven reservable sites through the Mistix Reservation System, 1-800-283-CAMP. Fishing, hiking, and riding. Elevation 2,400 feet. Fee.

Fish Lake—Thirty-three miles northwest of Cle Elum via County Road 903 and Forest Road 4330. Ten tent sites. Hunting, hiking, group camping.

Visitors bask in the sun beside the Cle Elum River in late summer. The river becomes a raging torrent during spring runoff. Forest Service photo.

Rafters drift down the Wenatchee River near Plain, Washington. Commercial rafting companies offer guided river trips. Forest Service photo.

Rough access road—no trailers. Elevation 3,400 feet.

Wishpoosh—Ten miles northwest of Cle Elum on County Road 903. Sixteen picnic sites, seventeen tent sites, and twenty-two tent/trailer units. Drinking water and boat launch. Water sports and fishing. Elevation 2,400 feet. Fee.

Owhi—Twenty-six miles northwest of Cle Elum via County Road 903 and Forest Road 46. Six picnic sites and twenty-two tent units, walk-in sites only. Fishing, swimming, boating, and trails. Elevation 2,800 feet.

Tamarack Spring—Twenty-six miles south of Cle Elum via Interstate 90 and forest roads 33, 3330, and 3120. Three tent/trailer units and drinking water. Horse riding and hunting. Elevation 4,700 feet.

Taneum—Twenty-one miles southeast of Cle Elum via Interstate 90 and Forest Road 33. Sixteen picnic sites, two tent units, thirteen tent/trailer units, and drinking water. Elevation 2,400 feet. Fee.

Beverly—Twenty-five miles north of Cle Elum via County Road 970 and Forest Road 9737. Thirteen tent units and three tent/trailer units. Mountain climbing, trails, horse riding. Elevation 3,200 feet.

Mineral Springs—Eighteen miles northeast of Cle Elum via U.S. Highway 97. Five tent units, seven tent/trailer units and drinking water. Fishing, hunting, berries, mushrooms, picnicking, and winter sports. Elevation 2,700 feet. Fee.

Buck Meadows—Thirty-six miles south of Cle Elum on Forest Road 31. Five tent/trailer units. Lightly developed. Riding horses. Elevation 4,200 feet.

Swauk—Twenty-two miles northeast of Cle Elum via U.S. Highway 97. Thirty-four picnic sites, twenty-three tent/trailer units, group picnic site, and drinking water. Fishing, mushrooms, hunting, and cross-country skiing. Elevation 3,200 feet.

Haney Meadows—Twenty-six miles northeast of Cle Elum via U.S. Highway 97 and Forest Road 9712. Sixteen tent/trailer units. Horse trails, hunting, and mountain biking. Elevation 5,100 feet.

Ice Water—Twenty miles south of Cle Elum on Forest Road 33. Seventeen tent/trailer units. Motorcycle trails, fishing, and hunting. Elevation 2,400 feet.

Other Campgrounds

Lake Easton State Park
U-Fish and RV Park—Exit 63
RV Town—Easton

Resorts and Businesses
The towns of Cle Elum and Roslyn offer groceries, gas, and lodging. Cle Elum also offers museums, sports equipment rentals, and hunting and fishing licenses. Roslyn is a small mining town made famous as the location of the television show "Northern Exposure." It offers a museum, a bed and breakfast, a bicycle shop, and cross-country ski rentals. Snoqualmie Pass offers downhill skiing during the winter months and restaurants, gas, and lodging all year.

Resorts include Snoqualmie Pass Inn, Moore House Inn/Bed and Breakfast, Ma Ma Vallones Bed and Breakfast, Hidden Valley Guest Ranch, Mineral Springs Restaurant and Inn, The Last Resort, cabins, and rental equipment.

Naches Ranger District

Information Centers
Naches Ranger Station, 10061 Highway 12, Naches, WA 98937, (509) 653-2205 or (509) 965-8005 voice/TT. Staffed information desk, map and book sales, and restrooms.

Recreation Highlights
Mather Memorial Parkway—A scenic fifty-three-mile portion of Highway 410 that travels over Chinook Pass to Mount Rainier National Park and the Mount Baker-Snoqualmie National Forest.

Rimrock Lake—A large reservoir offering Forest Service campgrounds, picnic areas, swimming, boating, fishing, and views of surrounding mountains. Located off Highway 12 on the way to White Pass.

Boulder Cave—A 350-foot-long and thirty-foot-wide natural cave formed by a fracture in lava layers from an ancient volcanic eruption. An easy mile-long barrier-free trail leads to the cave mouth. Rare, big-eared bats live in the cave. Try not to disturb them. Carry two sources of light and wear boots and warm clothing to explore the cave.

Campgrounds
Windy Point—Thirteen miles west of Naches via U.S. Highway 12. Fifteen tent/trailer units and drinking water. Fishing and picnicking. Elevation 2,000 feet. Fee.

Willows—Nineteen miles west of Naches via U.S. Highway 12. Sixteen tent/trailer units and drinking water. RVs to twenty feet. Fishing and picnicking. Elevation 2,400 feet. Fee.

Wild Rose—Twenty miles southwest of Naches via U.S. Highway 12. Eight tent/trailer units and drinking water. Fishing and picnicking. Elevation 2,400 feet.

River Bend—Twenty-one miles southwest of Naches via U.S. Highway 12. Six tent/trailer units and drinking water. Fishing. Elevation 2,500 feet. Fee.

Hause Creek—Twenty-two miles southwest of Naches via U.S. Highway 12. Forty-two tent/trailer units, one barrier-free unit, and drinking water. Fishing. Elevation 2,500 feet. Fee.

South Fork Tieton—Twenty-seven miles southwest of Naches via U.S. Highway 12, County Road 1200, and Forest Road 1203. Unrestricted parking spaces will accommodate up to fifteen RVs to twenty feet. Swimming and fishing. Elevation 3,000 feet.

Indian Creek—Thirty-two miles southwest of Naches via U.S. Highway 12. Thirty-nine tent/trailer units and drinking water. Maximum trailer length thirty-two feet. Near Rimrock Lake. Elevation 3,000 feet. Fee.

Dog Lake—Twenty-two miles northeast of Packwood via U.S. Highway 12. Eleven tent/trailer units and RVs to twenty feet. Fishing, boating, and hunting. Elevation 3,400.

White Pass Lake—Nineteen miles northeast of Packwood via U.S. Highway 12. Sixteen tent/trailer units. Trailhead for Pacific Crest Trail, boating, and fishing. Elevation 4,500 feet.

White Pass Lake Horse Camp—Thirty-seven miles northeast of Packwood via U.S. Highway 12. Campsites and horse facilities. No boat motors and fly fishing only at Leech Lake. Elevation 4,500 feet.

Clear Lake—Thirty-seven miles southwest of Naches via U.S. Highway 12, County Road 1200, and Forest Road 1200-840. Four picnic sites, fifty-seven tent units, one group camp, and drinking water. Fishing and boating. Elevation 3,100 feet.

Peninsula—Twenty-six miles southwest of Naches off County Road 1200. Nineteen tent/trailer units. Boat launch, boating, fishing, waterskiing, and Rimrock Lake. Elevation 3,000 feet.

Cottonwood—Twenty-two miles northwest of Naches on State Highway 410. Sixteen tent/trailer units. Drinking water. Fishing. Elevation 2,300 feet. Fee.

Sawmill Flat—Twenty-five miles northwest of Naches on State Highway 410. Five picnic sites, twenty-five tent/trailer units, one barrier-free site, and drinking water. Fishing. Elevation 2,500 feet. Fee.

Little Naches—Twenty-six miles northwest of Naches on State Highway 410. Twenty-one tent/trailer units and drinking water. Fishing. Elevation 2,562 feet. Fee.

Kaner Flat—Thirty-two miles northwest of Naches via State Highway 410 and Forest Road 1900. Forty-two tent/trailer units, and drinking water. Six double and one triple unit will accommodate RVs up to thirty feet. Two picnic shelters will accommodate four families. One group reservation area. Motorcycle trails, group reservations. Elevation 2,600 feet. Fee.

Soda Springs—Thirty-eight miles northwest of Naches via Highway 410 and County Road 1800. Twenty-six tent/trailer sites and RVs to thirty feet. Drinking water. Fishing, geology, mineral springs. Elevation 3,100 feet. Fee.

Bumping Crossing—Forty-four miles northwest of Naches via State Highway 410 and County Road 1800. Twelve tent/RV units and RVs to twenty feet. Fishing and hiking. No vehicles on Bumping River shore within camp limits. Elevation 3,200 feet.

Bumping Lake—Forty-four miles northwest of Naches via State Highway 410 and County Road 1800. Forty-five tent/RV units and drinking water. Boating, fishing, and swimming. Elevation 3,400 feet. Fee.

Bumping Dam—Forty-three miles northwest of Naches via State Highway 410 and County Road 1800. Twenty-three tent/RV units, RVs to twenty-two feet. Fishing, boating, and sailing. Elevation 3,400 feet. Fee.

Halfway Flat—Twenty-eight miles northwest of Naches via State Highway 410 and Forest Road 1704. Eight campsites with six doubles and a triple to accommodate large RVs. Fishing and hiking. Elevation 2,500 feet.

Boulder Cave—Twenty-six miles northwest of Naches via State Highway 410 and Forest Road 1704. Picnic area. Fishing, hiking, and cave exploring. National Recreation Trail. Barrier-free facilities. Elevation 2,500 feet.

Indian Flat—Thirty-one miles northwest of Naches via State Highway 410. Eleven tent/trailer units, RVs to twenty feet, and drinking water. Fishing. Elevation 2,600 feet. Fee.

Cedar Springs—Thirty-three miles northwest of Naches via State Highway 410 and County Road 1800. Fifteen tent/RV units and drinking water. Fishing. Elevation 2,800 feet. Fee.

Lodgepole—Forty-five miles northwest of Naches via State Highway 410. Thirty-three tent/RV units and drinking water. Fishing and berry picking. Maximum trailer length, twenty feet. Elevation 3,500 feet. Fee.

Pleasant Valley—Forty-one miles northwest of Naches via State Highway 410. Four picnic sites, sixteen tent/RV units and drinking water. Fishing and hiking. Elevation 3,300 feet. Fee.

Hells Crossing—Thirty-eight miles northwest of Naches via State Highway 410. Eighteen tent/trailer units, RVs to twenty feet, and drinking water. Fishing and hiking. Elevation 3,250 feet. Fee.

Crow Creek—Thirty-two miles northwest of Naches via State Highway 410 and forest roads 1900 and 1904. Fifteen tent/trailer units and RVs to thirty feet. Hunting, fishing, and motorbiking. Elevation 2,900 feet.

Other Campgrounds and Facilities

The Cove Resort—Rimrock Lake, fifty campsites with full hookups. (509) 672-2470.

12 West Resort—Rimrock Lake, trailer units with hookups, boat landing, moorage. (509) 672-2460.

Silver Beach Resort—Rimrock Lake, fifty-three trailer units with dump station, adjacent to Forest Service campground. (509) 672-2500.

Squaw Creek Resort—Sixty RV sites with hookups and dump station. Tent camping, showers, cabins. 19.2 miles west of Naches Ranger Station. (509) 658-2926.

Bumping Lake Marina—Fifty-nine miles west of Yakima via Highway 12 and the Bumping Lake Road 1800 and Homes Road 1800394. Forty camping spaces with lights and water. Bathrooms available. Boat rentals.

Resorts and Businesses

White Pass offers restaurants, gas, minor car repair, towing service, groceries, fishing licenses, Sno-park permits, and lodging.

Indian Creek Corral—Horse rental, hour/day pack trips, hunting trips. (509) 672-2400.

White Pass Day Lodge/Ski Shop—Ski rentals. (509) 672-3106.

Chinook Pass offers restaurants, gas, groceries, and lodging.

Susee's Skyline Packers—Outfitter guide, big game hunting, summer wilderness adventures. July-November. (206) 472-5558.□

NOTES

Many visitors to the Wenaha-Tucannon Wilderness travel by horseback, especially during the fall hunting season. Forest Service photo.

UMATILLA NATIONAL FOREST

The Umatilla National Forest in the Blue Mountains encompasses a series of tree-covered lava plateaus cut by stream canyons. Much of the 300,000 acres located in Washington State lie within the 177,465-acre Wenaha-Tucannon Wilderness.

Hunting and wilderness hiking are the most popular recreation uses of this remote area. The national forest is far from urban areas and the other national forests in Washington. The rustic campgrounds, clear rivers, and little-used trails offer many chances for quiet, low-stress recreational experiences.

Location

The Umatilla National Forest straddles the state line between Washington and Oregon in the southeastern corner of Washington. Visitors from the north and west reach the national forest via highways 12 and 11 from Yakima and Walla. Those from the south and east access the forest via Highway 84 in Oregon.

Climate

Climate varies markedly with elevation within the national forest. The lava plateaus at 8,000 feet receive much more rain and have cooler temperatures than the canyon bottoms at 1,600 feet. Precipitation varies from thirty to almost seventy inches.

Changes in weather are common, but summers are generally warm and dry with cool evenings. Winters are cold and snowy. Springs and falls are usually mild.

Geology

The lava plateaus of southeastern Washington are part of the Columbia River Plateau, a series of hundreds of lava flows that erupted from vents in the ground around six to sixteen million years ago. The basalt lava was very hot and fluid and may have flowed as fast as thirty miles per hour. The lava spread all over eastern Washington and parts of eastern Oregon, burying almost all previously existing landforms.

Rivers have cut down through the lava, creating steep-sided canyons whose walls show the lava layers stacked up like pancakes up to 200 feet thick.

Ecology

Umatilla National Forest ecosystems vary with elevation and precipitation. The high-elevation lava plateaus grow ponderosa and lodgepole pine forests, which provide habitat for elk, deer, bighorn sheep, mountain lion, hoary marmot, and other large mammals. Mountain meadow plants include juniper, pink Douglas onion, golden lupine, blue camas, and yellow balsam root.

The lower-elevation, canyon-bottom plant communities rely on the water provided by the rivers and streams. Streamside plant communities may include licorice and maidenhair fern, wild ginger, and phantom orchids.

UMATILLA NATIONAL FOREST

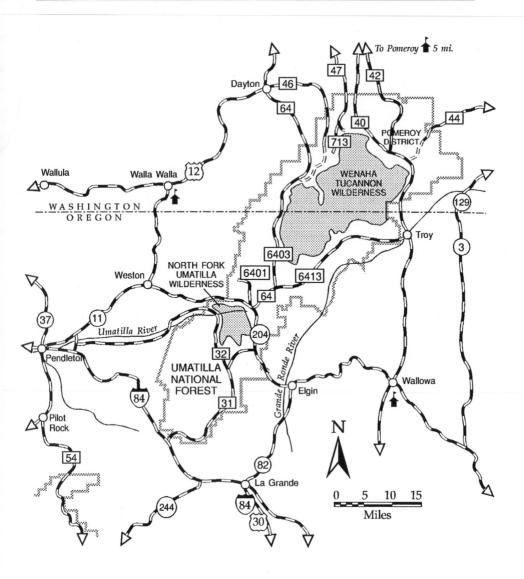

To Pomeroy 5 mi.

Dayton
46
64
47
42
40
44
713
POMEROY
DISTRICT
WENAHA
TUCANNON
WILDERNESS

Wallula
Walla Walla
12
129

WASHINGTON
OREGON

Troy
3

6403

NORTH FORK
UMATILLA
WILDERNESS
Weston
6401
6413
64

Umatilla River
204

37
11

32

Pendleton
UMATILLA
NATIONAL
FOREST
Grande Ronde River
Elgin
Wallowa

84
31

Pilot
Rock

54

82

N

La Grande

0   5   10   15
Miles

244
84
30

Yellow warblers and red-eyed vireos may perch in the trees.

History

The area we know as the Umatilla National Forest was once home to the Nez Perce, Cayuse, and Umatilla Indians, and modern-day members of the tribes still use the area today. One translation of the Indian name "Umatilla" gives the meaning as "water rippling over sand," a reference to the clear, fish-rich rivers that flow through the canyons. Many prehistoric trails cross the forest. Ancient campsites along these trails are more than 8,000 years old.

In the 1800s, miners and fur-trappers visited the area looking for riches, and pioneers passed through on the Oregon Trail on their way west. A few homesteaders made their homes here and towns sprang up along the rivers and travel routes. The Indians were relegated to reservations, some nearby and others many hundreds of miles away.

Forest-wide Recreation Opportunities in Washington

Scenic Drives

Forest Road 40—Panoramic views of the Blue Mountains, the Wenaha-Tucannon Wilderness, Eagle Cap, and Wallowa mountains in Oregon and the Seven Devils in Idaho. Take Forest Road 40, which begins fifteen miles south of Pomeroy, Washington, off County Road 128. Closed in winter.

Kendall Skyline Road—Starts in Dayton, Washington, on Forest Road 64. Offers spectacular vistas of canyons, mountains, timber, and the Columbia River. Closed in winter.

Wild and Scenic Rivers

The Wenaha River was designated a Wild and Scenic River in 1988 to recognize and to help protect its free-flowing beauty and the integrity of its ecosystems.

The river flows east for twenty miles from the Wenaha Forks where the north and south forks join to form the main Wenaha. It empties into the Grande Ronde River at Troy, Oregon. The river is located almost entirely within the Wenaha Tucannon Wilderness.

Wilderness Areas

Wenaha-Tucannon Wilderness—contains more than 177,460 acres of lava plateaus and the deep canyons of the Wenaha and Tucannon rivers. Elevations range from 2,000 to 6,400 feet. The wilderness is popular with hunters, anglers, and backpackers.

Wildlife

The forest supports one of the largest herds of Rocky Mountain elk in the nation. An estimated 22,000 elk roam the forest and an estimated 30,000 elk hunters stalk them each fall. Other large mammals include white-tailed deer, bighorn sheep, and mountain lion. Bald eagles and peregrine falcons, both endangered species, are sometimes seen within the national forest.

Desert bighorn sheep were introduced to the national forest by the Washington Department of Wildlife in the 1960s. Their population has

Large Populations of elk and deer provide many opportunities for wildlife watching and hunting within the Umatilla National Forest. Forest Service photo.

increased to 120 animals. Rocky Mountain bighorn sheep have also been transplanted to the area by the Oregon Department of Fish and Wildlife and the Washington Department of Wildlife. This herd appears to be threatened by a disease and winter competition with a large elk herd.

Northern Pacific rattlesnakes live in the Umatilla National Forest. The snakes are more likely to be out in early morning and late evening. Rattlesnakes are wary of humans and will usually slither away and hide.

If you encounter a snake step back slowly, make as little movement as possible and yell for help. Rattlesnakes can't hear above-ground sounds, but they are sensitive to vibrations and temperature changes. Wear boots and carry a long stick to tap rocks. Never stick your foot or hand under a rock or any place you can't see. If you are bitten soak the bite area in cold water and get medical attention. People very rarely die from rattlesnake bites.

Wildlife Viewing

W. T. Wooten Wildlife Area—Contains 11,185 acres, mostly on the northwest boundary of the national forest near Dayton, Washington. This area has Rocky Mountain elk, deer, bighorn sheep, black bear, cougar, bobcat, cottontail and snowshoe rabbit, ruffed and blue grouse, valley and mountain quail, and chukar, and Hungarian partridge.

Grouse Flats Wildlife Area—640 acres on a bench six miles south of Mount Misery adjacent to the Wenaha Tucannon Wilderness. The area is a vital calving ground for elk and also supports deer, bear, bighorn sheep, and other mammals and birds.

Asotin Creek Wildlife Area—10,416 acres about thirteen miles south-west of Asotin. Elk winter range and calving area. Chukar partridge habitat and excellent early summer trout fishing.

Hunting

Seasons open each year for white-tailed and mule deer, Rocky Mountain elk, bighorn sheep, black bear, and mountain lion. The forest is heavily hunted. It is the busiest recreation season of the year. Washington State hunting license required. The Wenaha-Tucannon Wilderness offers notable wilderness elk hunting.

Fishing

The Grand Ronde, Wenaha, Tucannon, and Touchet rivers and their tributaries offer good fishing. Species include steelhead, chinook salmon, and rainbow trout. Washington fishing license required.

Foraging

Huckleberry picking and mushrooming are popular activities within the national forest. Berries ripen mid-summer and mushrooms are best in the fall. The Forest Service offers field guides to help identify edible plants. Prices are under $10 and they are sold in most Forest Service information offices.

Firewood cutting is permitted outside the wilderness. Wood can be gathered for campground use free of charge, but permits are necessary to cut several cords for home use.

Water Sports

Whitewater rafting and canoeing can be enjoyed on the Grande Ronde River. Permits are not required for individuals or private groups. Outfitters, guides, and shuttle services are available.

Winter Sports

Downhill Skiing

Ski Bluewood—Located twenty-one miles southeast of Dayton, Washington. The area offers twenty-six runs, two chairlifts, one platter pull, a day lodge, ski equipment rental, and a ski school. Sno-park permits are required and available at the day lodge.

Cross-country Skiing

Skiers use many miles of snow-covered forest roads. Access to plowed state highway turnouts is provided through Washington Sno-Park permits, available at local businesses and the Washington State Parks and Recreation Commission.

Sample ski trip: **Iron Springs Road**—From Clarkston, Washington, take County Road 128 south to Peola, Washington. Take first left onto Ruchert Road, then first left on Iron Springs Road 42. Well-groomed route along a snow-covered forest road from December through March. Used by skiers and snowmobilers. Leads to Clearwater Lookout at 5,658 feet. Eight miles.

Snowmobiling

Snowmobilers use hundreds of miles of forest roads and 200 miles of groomed trails centered near Mount Misery and Touchet. The trails are groomed by active snowmobile clubs.

Snowmobile riders enjoy snow-covered roads and trails during the winter within the Umatilla National Forest. Forest Service photo.

Sample Snowmobile Route: **Kendall Skyline Road**—From Dayton, Washington, follow "Ski Bluewood" signs to Sno-park located at Touchet Corral. Difficult route over twenty-four miles of snow-covered forest road. No wheeled traffic allowed on groomed trail.

Off-road Vehicles

Hundreds of miles of forest roads are open to wheeled and motorized vehicles. All trails within the wilderness area are open only for hikers and horses. Some trails outside the wilderness area are available for trail motorcycle riding.

Off-road-vehicle trails include the Meadow Creek Trail and a four-mile ATV route off the Kendall Skyline Road at Godman.

Mountain Bikes

Mountain Bike Trails in the national forest include Kendall Skyline Road, Jungle Spring Trail, and Tuccanon River Trail.

Backcountry Travel

More than 300 miles of trail in the national forest in Washington are open for hikers, backpackers, and horseback riders. Trails offer a variety of difficulty levels.

Forest Service information centers offer complete listings of trails in the national forest. The following are just samples of the many opportunities available.

Non-Wilderness Trail

Wenatchee Trail—this steep, rocky, three-mile trail is maintained for hikers and horses only. The trail offers beautiful views of the Wenatchee drainage, the snow-covered Wallowa Mountains, and Seven Devil Mountains. At the valley bottom, Wenatchee Creek offers abundant water and plenty of camping. Accessed via County Road 128 from Pomeroy, Washington. Continue straight on Forest Road 40 to Troy Junction (about seventeen miles). Take Forest Road 44 for three miles and Forest Road 43 for two miles. Trail takes off on the right.

Wilderness Trail

Oregon Butte Trail—located within the Wenaha-Tucannon Wilderness, this three-mile trail climbs across a ridge and descends through a saddle toward Oregon Butte. From a log water trough, the trail then climbs to Oregon Butte Lookout. This trail is heavily traveled during hunting seasons. It is one of the first areas to be hit by snow in the fall. Take the Eckler Mountain Road from Dayton, Washington for about fifteen miles. At the stone monument at a "Y" in the road, turn right on Kendall Skyline Road 46 and drive for twelve miles to Godman Guard Station. Turn left on Forest Road 4608. Take all main right turns for five miles to Teepee trailhead. Party size in wilderness areas limited to twelve people and eighteen head of stock.

Horse Trail

Panjab Trail—well-maintained trail open to hikers and horses; accesses the Wenaha-Tucannon Wilderness. Located twelve miles east of Dayton, Washington, on Forest Road 4713. The trail follows a gentle incline along

Panjab Creek for the first three miles. It then climbs for two miles to the Indian Corral where the trail levels out on a ridge top. The trailhead offers loading docks, hitching rails, and feed mangers. Water is readily available, but feed is scarce due to cattle grazing, so carrying feed is advisable.

Mountain Climbing

Rock climbers can scale the vertical cliffs in the river canyons, but the basalt rock is very crumbly and climbing is dangerous.

Barrier-free Sites

All Forest Service information offices and restrooms are barrier free, and some trailheads, including Meadow Creek, Teepee, and Elk Flat, offer barrier-free restrooms.

Forest Headquarters

Umatilla National Forest Headquarters, 2517 W. Hailey Ave., Pendleton, OR 97801, (503) 276-3811.

Ranger District Recreation Opportunities

Pomeroy Ranger District

The Pomeroy Ranger District is the most northern district in the Umatilla National Forest. Most of the Washington portion of the forest lies within the Pomeroy District. The lava plateaus and canyons of the Wenaha-Tucannon Wilderness make up most of the ranger district.

Information Centers

Pomeroy Ranger Station, Rt. 1, Box 53-f, Pomeroy, WA 99347, (509) 843-1891. Staffed information desk, map and book sales, and restrooms.

Recreation Highlights

Clearwater Lookout and Heliport—Built in 1935, this ninety-nine-foot-high tower offers bird's eye views of the Wenaha-Tucannon Wilderness. Located on Forest Road 40, twenty-five miles south of Pomeroy.

Kendall Skyline Road—Forest Road 64 offers spectacular views of the area. Started as a private road prior to World War I and completed by the Civilian Conservation Corps in 1930. Dedicated in 1950.

Campgrounds in Washington

Alder Thicket—Twenty miles south of Pomeroy on Forest Road 40. Two tent units and four tent/trailer units, RVs to sixteen feet. Hunting. Elevation 5,100 feet.

Big Springs—Twenty-three miles south of Pomeroy on Forest Road 42. Five picnic sites and six tent units. Hunting. Elevation 5,000 feet.

Godman—Twenty-five miles southeast of Dayton on Forest Road 46. One picnic site, three tent sites, four tent/trailer units and RVs to sixteen feet. Hunting, trailhead, horse facilities. Elevation 6,050 feet.

Teal Spring—Twenty-six miles south of Pomeroy on Forest Road 40. Five picnic sites, five tents sites and three tent/trailer units. Hunting and scenic views. Elevation 5,600 feet.

Tucannon—Twenty five miles south of Pomeroy on Forest Road 47. Six picnic sites, one tent unit, five tent/trailer units, and RVs to sixteen feet. Hunting, fishing, and hiking. Elevation 2,600 feet.

Wickiup—Thirty four miles south of Pomeroy via Forest Roads 40 and 44. Six picnic sites, one tent unit, eight tent/trailer units, and RVs to sixteen feet. Hunting and scenic views. Elevation 5,800 feet.

Other Campgrounds

Lewis and Clark State Park, four miles east of Waitsburg on Highway 12, thirty campsites. Fee.

Fields Spring State Park, 4.5 miles south of Anatone on Highway 129, twenty campsites. Fee.

Outfitter Services

Blue Mountain Outfitters, Asotin, WA 99402;
Susee's Skyline Outfitters, Tacoma, WA 98404 (206) 972-5558;
Outback Ranch Outfitters, Joseph, OR 97846 (503) 426-4037;
Eagle Cap Pack Station, Joseph, OR 97846 (503) 432-9145.

Walla Walla Ranger District

The Walla Walla Ranger District is bounded by the Wenaha-Tucannon Wilderness to the north, the Umatilla Indian Reservation to the west, Highway 84 to the south, and the Grande Ronde River to the east. Although this ranger district is based in Washington State, most of its recreation opportunities lie across the border in Oregon.

Information Centers

Walla Walla Ranger Station, 1415 West Rose, Walla Walla, WA 99362, (509) 522-6290. Staffed information desk, map and book sales, and restrooms.

Campgrounds

All Walla Walla District campgrounds are in Oregon.□

ADDITIONAL INFORMATION

Guided Trips

Interested in guided explorations of Washington National Forests? The following organizations offer outdoor experiences that allow you to find out more in-depth information about wildlife, plants, geology, history, and other subjects.

North Cascades Institute
2105 Highway 20
Sedro Woolley, WA 98284
(206) 856-5700
Seminars, courses, and children's camps

Sierra Club
Cascade Chapter
1516 Melrose Ave.
Seattle, WA 98122
(206) 625-0632
Hiking and field trips

The Washington Native Plant Society
P.O. Box 576
Woodinville, WA 98072
Field trips and botany getaways

National Audubon Society
P.O. Box 462
Olympia, WA 98507
(206) 786-8020
Expeditions, field trips, seminars, and institutes

Cascade Orienteering Club
P.O. Box 31375
Seattle, WA 98103
(206) 783-3866
Cross-country walking or running

Washington State Outfitters and Guides Association

High Country Outfitters
22845 NE 8th, Suite 331
Redmond, WA 98053
(206) 392-4644
For river rafting call: (206) 234-4644

The Mountaineers
300 Third Ave. West
Seattle, WA 98119
(206) 284-6310
Outdoor education, recreation and adventure

Pacific Northwest Field Seminars

Northwest Interpretive Association
83 S. King St.
Suite 212
Seattle, WA 98104
(206) 553-2636
Outdoor courses from May-Sept.

Down Stream River Runners
12112 NE 195th
Bothell WA 98011
1-800-234-4644

Further Information and Resources

Call or write the following organizations for more in-depth information about a variety of aspects of Washington National Forests.

Washington State Parks and Recreation
7150 Clearwater Lane
P.O. Box 42662
Olympia, WA 98504-2662
Brochures and information on Sno-Parks, cross-country skiing and snowmobile recreation. State parks and facilities.

Washington State Winter Recreation Guide
(206) 623-3777
Information on winter recreation

Washington Trails Association
(206) 625-1367
Directory of where to find information on trail and road conditions, campsites, hiking and other recreational opportunities.

Cascade Ski Report
(206) 634-0200

Cross-Country Ski Report
(206) 632-2021

Pass Reports
1-900-407-7277

Ski Area Information
Snoqualmie Pass — (206)236-1600
Ski Bluewood — (509)382-2877
Crystal Mountain — (206)634-3771
49 Degrees North — (509)458-9208
Mount Baker — (206)374-1693
Stevens Pass — (206)634-1645
White Pass — (509)672-3100

North Cascades National Park
2105 Highway 20
Sedro Woolley, WA 98284
(206) 856-5700

Mount Rainier National Park
Information Center
915 Second Ave.
Seattle, WA 98104
(206) 553-0170

Washington State Ferries
801 Alaskan Way
Seattle, WA 98104-1487
(206) 84-FERRY

Olympic National Park
600 East Park Ave.
Port Angeles, WA 98362
(206) 452-5401

Charters and Tours
Gray Line of Seattle
720 S. Forest St.
Seattle, WA 98134
(206) 624-5813

Cascade Trailways
2209 Pacific Ave.
Tacoma, WA 98402
(206)838-3465

Creative Tours of Washington
1030 A Ave.
Edmonds, WA 98020
(206) 771-4721

ABOUT THE AUTHOR

Wendy Walker works as a consultant for the U.S. Forest Service and other government agencies, creating educational exhibits and programs. She also teaches university courses in environmental education and works with schools to develop environmental education programs and teacher training.

Wendy is the author of *Washington National Forests*, a photo-essay book published by Falcon Press. She has also published magazine articles, essays, environmental education curricula, and environmental education dramas.☐